Creative
CARD MAKING
for Scrapbookers

226 IDEAS AND TECHNIQUES FOR HANDCRAFTED CARDS

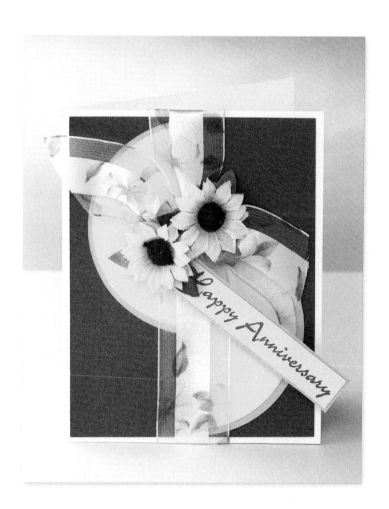

**MEMORY
MAKERS
BOOKS**

Executive Editor Kerry Arquette   *Founder* Michele Gerbrandt

Associate Editor Emily Curry Hitchingham

Art Director Andrea Zocchi

Graphic Designer Nick Nyffeler

Art Acquisitions Editor Janetta Abucejo Wieneke

Craft Editor Jodi Amidei

Photographer Ken Trujillo

Contributing Photographers Brenda Martinez, Jennifer Reeves

Digital Artist Jennifer Reeves

Art Caption Writer Torrey Miller

Editorial Support Karen Cain, MaryJo Regier, Lydia Rueger, Dena Twinem

Contributing Memory Makers Masters Valerie Barton, Susan Cyrus, Lisa Dixon, Kathy Fesmire, Brandi Ginn, Diana Graham, Diana Hudson, Torrey Miller, Kelli Noto, Denise Tucker, Andrea Lyn Vetten-Marley, Holle Wiktorek

Published by Memory Makers Books, an imprint of F+W Publications, Inc.
12365 Huron Street, Suite 500, Denver, CO 80234
Phone (800) 254-9124
First edition. Printed in the United States.
08 07 06 05 04 5 4 3 2 1

Library of Congress Cataloging-in-Publication Data

Creative card making for scrapbookers : 250 ideas and techniques for handcrafted cards.--
1st ed.
    p. cm.
Includes bibliographical references and index.
ISBN 1-892127-43-1
1. Greeting cards. 2. Scrapbooks. I. Memory Makers Books.

TT872.C72 2004
745.594--dc22

2004057879

Distributed to trade and art markets by
F+W Publications, Inc.
4700 East Galbraith Road, Cincinnati, OH 45236
Phone 1-800-289-0963

ISBN 1-892127-43-1
Memory Makers Books is the home of *Memory Makers*, the scrapbook magazine dedicated to educating and inspiring scrapbookers. To subscribe, or for more information, call (800) 366-6465.
Visit us on the Internet at www.memorymakersmagazine.com.

This book belongs to

_____

Special thanks to those product manufacturers who graciously supplied materials for the creation of projects featured throughout this book. Thanks also to our endlessly creative Memory Makers contributors for sharing their beautiful cards, which will undoubtedly inspire other scrapbookers to explore card making as a craft endeavor.

4 *table of contents*

Chapter 1 *Holidays*

Chapter 2 *Birthdays*

Introduction

We've all been there. Overwhelmed by the rows and rows of greeting cards tucked inside their staggered slots. We pick haphazardly from the array before us, each time hoping to find the perfect personal sentiment with just the right look. Maybe we'll find a card with a nice design but an unappealing sentiment, or one with a nice sentiment but an unappealing design. Often we simply settle for a card that "will do" because we feel overwhelmed and unconvinced at the prospect of finding that diamond in the rough.

By creating our own handmade cards, we can be sure both the design and sentiments are the jewels we intended because our emotions and creativity crafted them. In this age of electronic mail and hurried, commercialized communication, the lucky recipient of a handmade card will undoubtedly value the meaning represented by such a uniquely personal gesture.

Creative Card Making for Scrapbookers is the perfect resource for crafters looking to utilize their talents, tools, techniques and products in a new and meaningful way. Now your affinity for paper craft, embellishments and composition may be put to wonderful use in the form of beautiful handcrafted cards, invitations and announcements.

You will surely be inspired by this gallery of innovative and versatile card ideas, which can be adapted to any event and occasion all the year through. Detailed, illustrated step-by-step instructions and supply lists ensure that whether you are a card-creating aficionado or all new to the craft, your salutations will be successes when it comes time to sign, seal and deliver.

Make those uninspired store-bought card searches a thing of the past by creating artful keepsakes your friends and loved ones will cherish and keep. In personally crafting cards that acknowledge the special moments in life, we leave our signatures not only within a card's interior, but also in the effort and thoughtfulness that went into its creation.

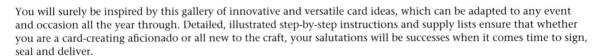

Michele Gerbrandt
Founding Editor
Memory Makers magazine

Getting Started

Why make your own cards?

Apart from being a natural extension of scrapbooking for its shared products and tools, card making is a rewarding creative endeavor with numerous artistic and economic benefits. For example:

Handmade cards make artful use of paper scraps, leftover embellishments and other "miscellaneous" items from your craft workspace and around the house.

Store-bought cards range in price from $0.38-$10.00, with the average card retailing between $2.00-$4.00. A typical U.S. household purchases 35 cards annually, making buying greeting cards over creating them quite expensive.

The average person receives more than 20 commercial greeting cards each year, rendering a handmade card a particularly thoughtful and unique treasure.

Personal correspondence such as greeting cards are the pieces of mail people most look forward to receiving, open first and keep for extended periods of time as keepsakes. Handmade cards enjoy a particularly long shelf life not only for the gestures they represent, but also because they are small works of art.

In crafting handmade cards, you will never risk sending a card identical to others a recipient may receive.

Customized handcrafted cards make it easy to express exactly what you wish to say because you act as both artist and writer.

Few store-bought cards can match the satisfaction achieved in creating and exchanging a handmade greeting.

Basic Card Construction

You can create customized cards entirely from scratch or you can get a jump-start by making use of pre-made blank card and envelope sets which may be purchased in various shapes, sizes and colors. Either approach offers widespread possibilities and ultimately depends on your time available and the particulars of your design. You'll first need to determine what size you wish your card to be. United States Postal Service regulations require that a piece be no smaller than 3½ x 5" for mailing. Square cards of any size, regardless of weight, require additional postage. For customized envelopes, utilize the patterns provided on pages 124-125 or choose from a wide array of manufactured templates.

Cut to desired size. Using a ruler, locate the central fold line; mark both sides. Align ruler with marks and score.

Fold card and apply pressure with a bone folder to create a sharp crease.

Basic Tools and Supplies

Card making incorporates countless tools from your scrapbooking collection. While tried-and-true staples serve as a foundation, this craft invites further exploration into uncharted creative territory. Sewing machines, hot irons, sandpaper and baking molds share craft table space with traditional standbys like cardstock and rubber stamps. In creating handmade cards, you'll call upon tools and supplies that span an inspired and limitless spectrum. Here is but a sampling of the essentials:

1. Paper: The foundation of your card base. While you may choose from an endless assortment of handmade, textured, patterned, tissue, parchment, corrugated and translucent papers, you'll want to be sure your card base is substantial. Cardstock makes for a particularly sturdy base. Layering thinner papers can also add thickness.

2. Paper trimmer: Create crisp, straight edges with the use of different interchangeable blades.

3. Scissors: Employ standard, decorative and fine-tip scissors for basic, elegant and detailed cuts.

  Bone folder: Useful for scoring and folding sharp creases.

  Craft knife: Essential for clean, intricate cuts. May also be used to lightly score a crisp fold.

4. Punches: Quick design additions available in numerous shapes and sizes.

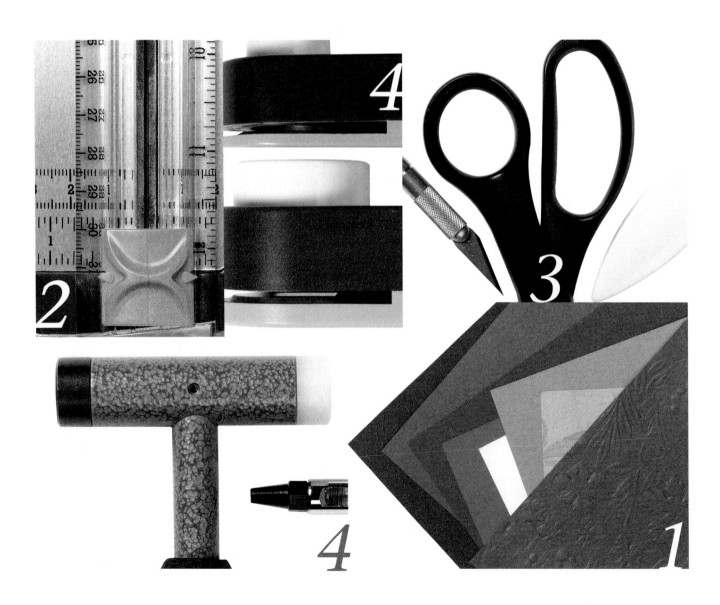

5. *Metal-edge ruler:* Use to make perfectly straight cuts with a craft knife in place of plastic rulers that can become damaged with gouges and nicks.

Stylus: Create embossed designs using stencils and a light table.

6. *Adhesives:* These include double-sided dispenser tabs, dimensional foam spacers, sheet adhesives, clear mounting tape, glue dots, jeweler's glue, glue pens, sticks, spray adhesive and decoupage adhesive. Double-sided dry adhesives prevent bulk while dimensional adhesives add elevation. Glue dots and jeweler's glue securely hold items such as wire, charms, metals and baubles to numerous surfaces, and glue pens and sticks are ideal for tidily applying adhesive to surfaces with ease. Spray adhesives secure fabrics and mount vellum and tissue papers invisibly while decoupage glues are ideal for assembling collages. Adhesive application machines easily transform an assortment of items into stickers.

7. *Heat tool:* Melt embossing powder sprinkled over a freshly stamped image to form a raised design.

8. *Stamps and ink:* Experiment with images, backgrounds, textures, frames and alphabets in rubber, sponge and foam stamping forms. Dye-based inks are quick-drying and are suitable for most paper surfaces, including vellum. Pigment inks dry more slowly, and may be used for heat embossing.

9. *Die cuts:* Utilize a die-cut machine and its various dies for cards, envelopes and innumerable decorative shapes.

All the Extras

Cards are created to be given away. Therefore the longevity and archival quality concerns of scrapbooking are typically not the same for handcrafted cards. In selecting accents, consider whether you wish to create a simple or more elaborate card based upon whether it will be reproduced several times or stand alone as a keepsake craft. Reproductions of original photos and memorabilia should be used when such are chosen as design additions. If you will be sending your card though the mail, weight and any irregular bulk should also be assessed, in which case lining an envelope with bubble wrap will help protect more delicate creations. Ultimately anything from outdated jewelry, around-the-house items and vintage magazine images may be used as artful additions in combination with any number of popular accents listed below.

1. Textiles: Enhance any card with eye-catching fabrics, fibers, ribbons, embroidery floss, zippers and machine or hand stitching for added texture.

2. Baubles: Include buttons, beads, glass marbles, rhinestones, gems, sequins, tiles and other out-of-the-ordinary embellishments for artful additions.

3. Organics: Showcase elements from the outdoors such as clay, pressed flowers, leaves, jute, hemp string, raffia, leather, mica, feathers, tiny shells and more.

4. Metals: For added impact, incorporate metal accent pieces, malleable sheets, mesh screen, or shape wire with the use of pliers, wire cutters, peg boards and coiling rods.

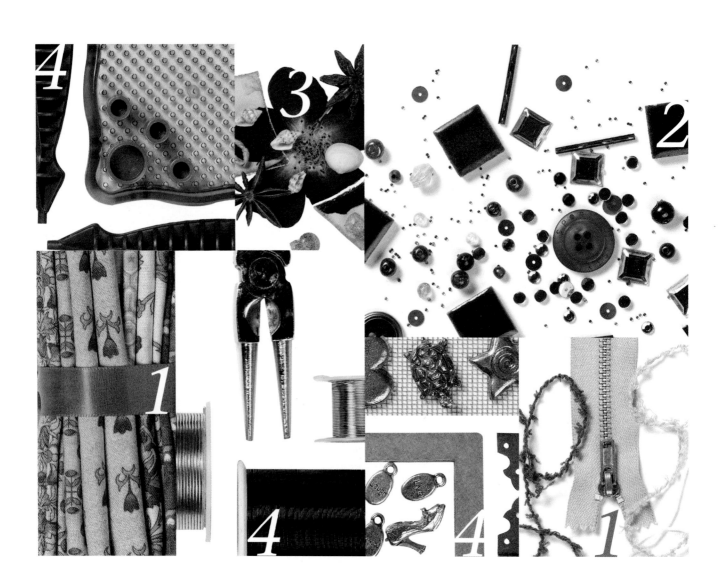

5. *Brads, snaps and eyelets:* Incorporate these fashionable fasteners for artistic flare alone or to affix items to your card base.

6. *Paint:* Acrylic and watercolor paints provide artful colorants. Test papers beforehand to assess how the paper will take the application, thereby discovering any potential warping, rippling or other possible distortions.

7. *Pens:* Write, highlight, color and add detail with pens and markers. Felt-tip, broad-point, fine-point, gel and metallic pens offer innumerable ways to add impact to any design.

8. *Chalk:* Use to age, shade or to add subtle coloration and detail.

9. *Stickers:* Quick and easy additions to dress up any design imaginable. Create your own with sheet adhesives, stamps and the like, or choose from countless manufactured images.

Holidays

chapter **1**

New Year's Greetings

Incorporate a little sparkle into a New Year's salutation. Start with a horizontally folded card base of iridescent white cardstock. Cut two rectangles of iridescent light blue and darker blue cardstocks. Layer and tear in half diagonally; discard one of each. Ink torn edges with blue stamping ink and mount. Print salutation on iridescent white cardstock; tear to size and ink edges. Mat salutation with mylar; affix to card with foam adhesive. Sandwich tinsel strands between salutation block and card front. For date, place foil sheet on cardstock and cover with number template. Trace numbers with hot pen according to manufacturer's directions. Tear date to size; mat with mylar and adhere.

Michelle Pendleton, Colorado Springs, Colorado

Supplies: White, light blue, and darker blue iridescent cardstocks (Golden Oak Papers); number template (Crafter's Workshop); hot foil pen and foil (Staedtler); mylar; fiber; blue stamping ink; foam spacers

Happy 2005

Send a warm and friendly salutation for the new year. Begin with vertically folded yellow card base. Treat edges with black ink. Cut rectangles from bright yellow cardstock, yellow vellum and striped patterned paper in various heights all as wide as card front; mount in layers across top half of card front. Adhere die-cut flower with foam adhesive, folding top of flower behind paper rectangle layers. Apply letter stickers to flower for sentiment. Print date on white cardstock, cut out individual numbers and adhere.

Susan Cyrus, Broken Arrow, Oklahoma

Supplies: Patterned paper (Chatterbox); letter stickers (EK Success); daisy die cut (Paper House Productions); black stamping ink; buff vellum; foam spacers; yellow, white and bright yellow cardstocks

Will You Be My Valentine?

Who could resist the face of this cute little cherub? Begin with a vertically folded piece of black cardstock. Adhere red handmade paper rectangles to left and bottom of card front. Mount photo in upper right corner. Adhere woven sayings at askew angles beside photo. Apply white acrylic paint to metal-rimmed vellum tag. Print title on transparency. Secure printed transparency to tag with eyelets. Tie ribbon through eyelets and adhere beneath photo. Accent metal letter tag and stamped tag with red ribbon. Create polymer clay heart accent by stamping into clay; bake as directed and paint when cooled. Assemble plastic letter and other letter elements to form word and adhere with foam spacers.

Brandi Ginn, Lafayette, Colorado

Supplies: Red handmade paper (Nature's Handmade Paper); plastic letter (K & Company); woven labels, vellum tag (Me & My Big Ideas); metal tag and letter (Making Memories); small circle metal tag (Magic Scraps); letter stamp and heart stamp (Hero Arts); polymer clay; red and white acrylic paints; red and gingham ribbon; foam spacers; transparency, eyelets; black cardstock

XOXO

Use photo-editing software to create this "cheeky" valentines card. Start with a long vertically folded red cardstock base. Layer with patterned paper. Manipulate photo in an editing program and print on regular paper. Lightly sand edges of photo and stamp with date stamp. Mat photo on red cardstock and adhere. Stamp letter stamps along bottom of photo. Print sentiment onto white cardstock; mat on red cardstock. Add decorative heart brad and adhere.

Carrie O'Donnell, Newburyport, Massachusetts

Supplies: Patterned paper (7 Gypsies); letter stamps (Turtle Press); date stamp (Staples); black ink; heart brad (www.absolutelyeverything.com); printer paper; sandpaper; red cardstock

Supplies: Patterned paper (7 Gypsies); hinges (Making Memories); key and lock charms (source unknown); red velveteen paper (Wintech); word stamp (Stampabilities); black embossing powder; white and red stamping inks; playing cards; cardboard; fiber; fine tip marker; black and white cardstocks

Love Coupons

This card houses mini gift coupons for a lucky loved one to redeem. See instructions below for card base instructions. Accent by threading key charm on fiber, securing ends on back. Glue lock charm on right edge of embossed flap. For "coupons" sand several playing cards. Print or hand-write coupons on white cardstock; cut to size and ink edges with red ink. Adhere with patterned paper scraps. House playing card coupons under hinged flap in window. Cover back of card with black cardstock to complete.

Jennifer Ingle, Aurora, Colorado

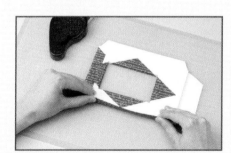

1 Cut a window into a piece of foam core board or corrugated cardboard. Cut patterned paper into a rectangle large enough to wrap base. Using a craft knife, cut an X from corner to corner in paper over window opening. Fold flaps around window to frame. Notch all corners and fold outside edges to back of base and adhere.

2 Line window opening with red velvet paper. Cut piece of black cardstock slightly larger than window for flap; layer with red velvet paper. Heat emboss center of velveteen paper with several coats of black embossing powder. While embossing powder still hot, ink stamp with white ink and stamp into hot embossing powder.

3 Using glue dots, affix one side of hinge to front side of embossed flap and the other side of hinge along left side of window opening.

Love

A heart of gold makes for an eye-catching card accent. Begin with a vertically folded red cardstock base. Cover front with flecked white cardstock. Stamp definition onto black cardstock using opaque white ink; tear in half. Hang key charm from gold thread; wrap torn cardstock and adhere to left side of card front. Cut heart from red cardstock; crumple, dab with embossing ink, emboss with gold powder and adhere. Stamp letters onto white cardstock. Cut into circles and place in binding discs. Cover with clear lacquer to seal; mount.

Vicki Garrett, Kingston, Ontario, Canada

Supplies: Definition and letter stamps (Stampin' Up!); binding discs (Rollabind); key charm (Magic Scraps); white, black and gold embossing inks; gold embossing powder; flecked white cardstock (Xpedx); black and red cardstocks

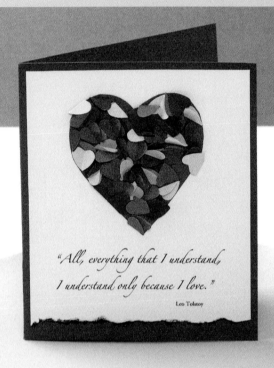

"All, everything that I understand, I understand only because I love."

Leo Tolstoy

...Because I Love

This card gives new meaning to a heart being "aflutter." Start with a vertically folded red cardstock base. Print sentiment onto textured cream cardstock. Tear edge, treat with black ink; and mount. Cut large heart from red cardstock; adhere. Punch tiny hearts from various shades of pink and red cardstocks. Fold punched hearts in half; apply glue to one side only and affix over large heart until covered.

Colleen Adams, Huntington Beach, California

Supplies: Textured cream cardstock (Club Scrap); heart punch (Family Treasures); black stamping ink; bright red, deep red, hot pink and pale pink cardstocks

My Heart Belongs To You

Create a charming, simply stated card. Begin with a base of horizontally folded black cardstock. Layer card front and interior with red cardstock. Cut white cardstock square; cover with patterned tissue paper and mat with black cardstock. Add metal frame, corners, sentiment and acrylic pebble. Wrap with gingham ribbon; add decorative clip and charm. Adhere assemblage to card front to complete.

Deanna Hutchison, Langley, British Columbia, Canada

Supplies: Metal frame, corners, clip, page pebble, metal phrase (Making Memories); patterned tissue (7 Gypsies); ribbon; heart charm; black and red cardstocks

Love

Show the one you love that you think he or she is cute as a button with this fun valentine card. Begin with a horizontally-folded textured pink cardstock card base. Cover card front with patterned paper. Cut out large heart from white cardstock; adhere to card front. Glue assorted red buttons over white cardstock heart. Accent card's corners with heart-shaped buttons. Print title on vellum and adhere to card front. Glue tiny pink rhinestones in corners to complete.

Amy McGovern, Eldersburg, Maryland

Supplies: Textured pink cardstock (Bazzill); patterned paper (K & Company); rhinestones (Mrs. Grossman's); buttons (Jo-Ann Fabric); vellum; white cardstock

Be Mine

Spell out your feelings for the one you love. Start with a vertically folded peach cardstock base. Stamp front of card with text stamp. Stamp cream suede paper and cut into diamond shape. Double mat with copper foil and cream cardstock; adhere. Embellish with skeleton leaves. Stamp rose on cream suede paper; cut to fit behind decorative frame and mount. Partially fill tiny bottle with beads. Roll small piece of patterned paper into scroll and tie with metallic floss. Insert scroll and seal with cork. Adhere wooden letter tiles for title. Tie fibers along card crease to complete.

Nicole LaCour, Memory Makers magazine

Supplies: Text stamp (My Sentiments Exactly); rose stamp (Biblical Impressions); wooden letter tiles, glass bottle (7 Gypsies); patterned paper (Me & My Big Ideas); metal frame (K & Company); metallic floss (DMC); skeleton leaves (Nature's Handmade Paper); copper foil (Heritage Handcrafts); fiber (Fiber Scraps); stamping ink (Tsukineko); cream suede paper (Wintech); peach and cream cardstocks

Happy St. Pat's Day

Any leprechaun would love this lucky card. Start with a horizontally folded card base of parchment-colored cardstock. Mat patterned paper with green cardstock and mount to card front. Thread shamrock buttons onto organza ribbon and adhere. Print sentiment onto white cardstock and tear into rough rectangle shape; chalk torn edges. Mat sentiment with green cardstock and mount to bottom of card front to finish.

Dolores Raml, Sioux Falls, South Dakota

Supplies: Patterned paper (source unknown); shamrock buttons (Jesse James); organza ribbon; green chalk; green, white and parchment-colored cardstocks

An Irish Blessing

Send someone you love a little "luck o' the Irish." Start with a horizontally folded textured dark green cardstock base. Stamp sentiment on textured cream cardstock and tear into random shape. Ink torn edges of sentiment with brown stamping ink and mount. Cut slit in card's crease; thread with gingham ribbon down left edge and accent with clover medallion.

Jill Tennyson, Lafayette, Colorado

Supplies: Sentiment stamp (River City Rubber Works); clover medallion (source unknown); textured cream and dark green cardstocks (Bazzill); black and brown stamping inks; gingham ribbon

Lucky Charm

A removable charm that you can wear adorns this festive St. Patrick's Day card. Start off with a horizontally folded textured green cardstock base. Use die-cut shamrock shape as a template; trace onto shrink plastic and cut out. Paint rough side with green acrylic paint; let dry. Punch hole in top of shamrock using a ¼" hole punch. Shrink according to manufacturer's directions and attach jump ring through hole. Apply iron-on adhesive to wrong side of fabric strip; cut to size and adhere with double-sided tape. Accent with shamrock charm attached by colored safety pin. Apply rub-on letters along bottom edge of card to finish.

Diana Hudson, Bakersfield, California

Supplies: Shrink plastic (K&B Innovations); shamrock die cut (Ellison); rub-on letters and colored safety pin (Making Memories); textured cardstock (Bazzill); green acrylic paint; fabric; jump ring; double-sided tape

Happy St. Patrick's Day

Clean lines and graphic design elements lend a modern feel to this card. Start with a vertically folded white cardstock base. Mat patterned paper with dark green paper and mount to card front. Layer with strip of striped paper matted on dark green cardstock. Print sentiment onto paper using a label maker font and green printer ink. Cut title into thin strip and adhere across bottom of card front to complete.

Kimberly Lund, Wichita, Kansas

Supplies: Patterned papers (Doodlebug Design); green and white cardstocks

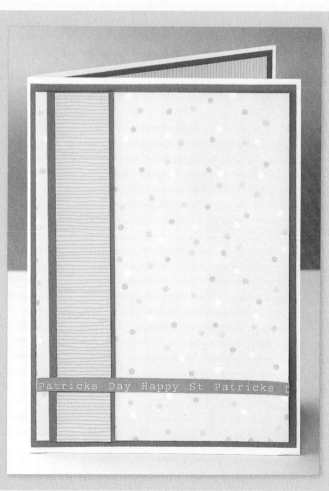

Happy Easter

Create an elegant Easter card with an accent made from air-dry clay. Start with a horizontally folded pink cardstock card base. Tear patterned paper slightly smaller than card, apply stickers and adhere. Sew along edges of patterned paper with sewing machine. For clay accent, roll out clay and stamp with inked rubber stamp. Cut into oval using template; poke holes in top for ribbon. Allow clay to dry according to manufacturer's instructions. Treat surface of dried plaque with pink chalk. Rub copper metallic rub-on pigment onto image. Color eye of rabbit with marker and accent with pompom tail. Thread ribbon through holes in accent and tie into bow. Attach brads to bottom left of card front. Hang accent with brad and affix accent to card front. Handwrite title on white cardstock and cut to fit concho. Color concho, brads, edge of accent and card edge with copper leafing pen.

Kari Hansen-Daffin, Memory Makers magazine

Supplies: Air-dry clay (Provo Craft) patterned paper (Me & My Big Ideas); rose stickers (Anna Griffin); rabbit stamp (Just For Fun Rubber Stamps); rub-on metallic copper (Craf-T); copper leafing pen (Krylon); concho (Scrapworks); gingham ribbon; oval template; round punch; white thread; pompom; brads; markers; copper stamping ink; pink and white cardstocks

...Chocolate Bunny

Capture the timeless art of eating that treasured chocolate bunny with this charming card. Begin with a long vertically folded card base of light brown cardstock. Layer card front with dark brown cardstock. Arrange and alter photos using a photo-editing program. Print photos on glossy photo paper and attach at askew angle to card front. Print sentiment on white cardstock; mat on light brown cardstock and mount at bottom to complete.

Carrie O'Donnell, Newburyport, Massachusetts

Supplies: Glossy photo paper; light brown, dark brown and white cardstocks

Hop Into Spring

This springtime wish is sure to generate a smile. Start with a horizontally folded sage green cardstock base. Mount striped green paper on front and back of card. Tear pink cardstock into rough rectangle and adhere. Apply acrylic letters to sage green cardstock strip. Adhere rabbit accent and title to card front. Make two small vertical cuts into top of card front; thread ribbon through. Tie ribbon in bow to complete.

Jennifer Troxell, Littleton, Colorado

Supplies: Patterned paper (source unknown); acrylic letters (K & Company); rabbit accent (Westrim); pink gingham ribbon; sage and pink cardstocks

Happy Easter

Create this artful and pretty Easter greeting in a pinch. Start with a long horizontally folded sage green cardstock card base. Mat patterned paper with purple cardstock and affix to card front. Adhere ribbon to strip of purple cardstock and mount on left side of card. Stamp sentiment on cardstock strips; add contrasting-colored circles on ends of both strips and create a hole in each with hole punch. Thread ribbon through holes and adhere to card front.

Tracy Miller, Fallston, Maryland

Supplies: Textured sage green, yellow and purple cardstocks (Bazzill); patterned paper, letter stamps (Wordsworth); ribbon; purple stamping ink

Easter Weaving

Strips of paper are woven together to create the look of an Easter basket on this pastel-pretty card. Start with a pre-scored pink card with precut window. Weave strips of four different patterned papers and adhere to card front around window. Punch two holes under window; tie organza ribbon through holes to form a French bow. Stamp rabbit image onto white cardstock; cut to size and mount in window on card's interior with foam spacers.

Kari Hansen-Daffin, Memory Makers magazine

Supplies: Pre-made card (Me & My Big Ideas); patterned paper (Current); rabbit stamp (100 Proof Press); plum stamping ink; hole punch; foam spacer; white and pink cardstocks

Mom

Shabby chic style makes for an elegant Mother's Day card. Start with a long, horizontally folded pink cardstock base. Dry brush with white acrylic paint to whitewash. Cut four rectangles from coordinating patterned papers; sand to distress. Adhere rectangles to card front and stitch with sewing machine. Adhere pearl beads to corners of card front. For tag element, sand pre-made tag and affix whitewashed die-cut letters and cameo; tie with ribbon accented with charms. Mount tag with foam adhesive to complete.

Jodi Amidei, Memory Makers Books

Supplies: Patterned papers (Anna Griffin); cameo, pearl beads, charms (Westrim); die-cut letters (QuicKutz); tag (Me & My Big Ideas); white acrylic paint; ribbon; foam spacers; pink cardstock

Mom

Show Mom her mothering surpasses even the June Cleaver-esque standards of the 1950s. Begin with horizontally folded white cardstock card base. Treat edges of card front with teal stamping ink. Cut gingham patterned paper rectangle and affix with decorative eyelets. Adhere vintage image onto patterned paper rectangle. Cut window in printed transparency, saving word; adhere over vintage image. Create title with letter stickers. Tie gingham ribbon on square buckle and adhere across bottom. Accent with pre-made quilled accents to complete.

Torrey Miller, Thornton, Colorado

Supplies: Patterned paper (Paper Adventures); printed transparency (Creative Imaginations); vintage image (DMD); quilled accents (EK Success); square buckle (7 Gypsies); heart eyelets (Eyelets Etc.); letter stickers (Wordsworth); gingham ribbon; teal stamping ink; white cardstock

Supplies: Patterned papers (Anna Griffin); green patterned paper and textured pink cardstock (Chatterbox); glass marbles

Mother's Day Bouquet

Give Mom a beautiful bouquet that will last for years to come. Create card base from horizontally folded textured pink cardstock. Use the instructions that follow to create patterned paper origami flowers. Arrange flowers and secure stems together with circular clip. Adhere flowers to card front. Cut thin strips of green patterned paper. Gently curl strips using edge of scissor blade as you would for curling ribbon; adhere. Print quote on green patterned paper; cut to size and adhere across bottom.

Torrey Miller, Thornton, Colorado

1 Cut five 3 x 3" squares of various patterned papers. Using a bone folder, fold in half diagonally; open and fold diagonally again from opposite corners. Turn and fold in half vertically. Open and fold again vertically from opposite corners.

3 Take center point edge and fold toward top.

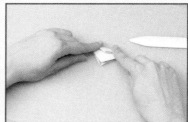

2 Fold diagonally; bring opposite corners to center, allowing folds to collapse into bottom square. Press to complete fold.

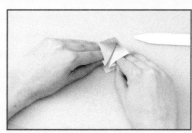

4 Pull top flap back to open square to form flower shape. Accent each "flower" center with glass pebble.

Mother

Layering select flowers gives this card dimension. Start by vertically folding embossed patterned paper. Cut individual flowers from glittered paper of identical design. Layer various-sized glittered flowers together to create layered effect; adhere to select flowers on card front. Affix woven label to pink tag. Ink edges of tag with green stamping ink. Tie ribbon around left edge of card front, securing tag through its hole.

Emily Curry Hitchingham, Memory Makers Books

Supplies: Embossed and glittered patterned paper (K & Company); woven label (Me & My Big Ideas); tag (Karen Foster Design); green stamping ink; ribbon; pink textured cardstock (Bazzill)

Mom

Paper tearing and curling combine to create these tole flowers. Start with a horizontally-folded base of textured pink cardstock. Cut 1" off bottom of card front. Treat edges with pink stamping ink. Using craft knife, cut four small horizontal slits through front and back of card, just down from folded edge. Thread gingham ribbon through slits and tie into knots. Layer pink and gingham ribbons and mount across bottom interior edge. Affix die-cut letters for title. Construct flowers by tearing several rough circles from yellow, orange and pink cardstocks in graduated sizes. Create rough petals by tearing and bending edges. Chalk tips of petals and apply touches of clear lacquer. Layer, adhere and accent with pre-threaded button stickers for centers.

Emily Curry Hitchingham, Memory Makers Books

Supplies: Button stickers (EK Success); die-cut letters (QuicK-utz); textured pink cardstock (Bazzill); gingham ribbon, pink ribbon; clear lacquer; chalk; pink stamping ink; pink, yellow and orange cardstocks

Dad

Incorporate the richness of copper metallic paper into a Father's Day card. Begin with a square card base of horizontally folded copper cardstock. Cover card front with ribbed rust cardstock. Affix smaller square of copper mesh with square copper brads. Apply wide copper tape across top. Stamp and emboss copper coffee cups on ribbed rust cardstock; tear to size and affix with copper brads. Adhere copper letters to ribbed rust cardstock; cut to size, cover with copper label holder and secure with brads.

Kari Hansen-Daffin, Memory Makers magazine

Supplies: Copper mesh and tape (Anima Designs); label holder (Nunn Design); letters (K & Company); square brads (Creative Impressions); stamp (Hampton Art Stamps); copper cardstock (Paper Adventures); ribbed rust cardstock (DMD); copper pigment ink; copper embossing powder

Supplies: Striped patterned paper (EK Success); map-patterned paper (Li'l Davis Designs); studs and concho (Scrapworks); rust and sand cardstocks

Best Dad In The World

Show your dad you think he's unsurpassed! Print sentiment on rust cardstock. Vertically fold card base from printed rust cardstock. Cut rectangle of striped patterned paper and adhere to card front. Affix decorative studs to corners of patterned paper on card front. Print part of title on sand cardstock. Cut smaller rectangle of map patterned paper and double mat with printed sand and rust cardstocks. Print sentiment on striped patterned paper; cut to size and insert in circular concho. Mount framed sentiment on square of rust cardstock and adhere to card front.

Jane Ecker, Batavia, New York

Dad, Love U

Create a masculine card with attractive coordinating papers. Start with a horizontally folded card base of textured brown cardstock. Mat patterned paper on textured navy cardstock and mount. Tear strip of striped paper, ink torn edges with brown stamping ink and adhere across card. Apply tag letter stickers to form sentiment. Affix snaps to tops of letter tags. Adhere letter stickers along bottom of torn strip to complete.

Linda Beeson, Ventura, California

Supplies: Patterned papers (Chatterbox); tag letter stickers (Sticker Studio); letter stickers (Me & My Big Ideas); snaps (Making Memories); textured navy and brown cardstocks (Bazzill); brown stamping ink

Dad

Any "do-it-yourselfer" dad will appreciate repurposed bathroom tiles on his Father's Day card. Begin with a horizontally folded white cardstock base. Create patchwork background by tearing a variety of green patterned papers and adhering them at random to card front. Layer with strip of colored mesh. Stamp image onto mica chip with solvent-based ink; adhere to lower left corner of card front. Apply letter squares to bathroom tiles with decoupage adhesive. Mount tiles with tacky tape. Tie fiber around top of card front to finish.

Kelli Noto, Centennial, Colorado

Supplies: Patterned papers, letter squares, mica chip (Hot Off The Press); fish stamp (source unknown); brown solvent ink (Tsukineko); mesh; bathroom tiles; decoupage adhesive; white cardstock

Happy Father's Day

Give a "man of few words" a definition-inspired sentiment to ponder. Begin with a card base of horizontally folded textured dark brown cardstock. Cover card front with light brown and medium brown cardstocks. Adhere gingham ribbon across card front where cardstocks meet. Cut saying from patterned paper; double mat on dark brown and black cardstocks. Mount sentiment in center of card front. Handwrite salutation on light brown cardstock; mat with black cardstock. Attach to card front with circular clip.

Supplies: Patterned paper (K & Company); textured dark brown cardstock (Bazzill); circular clip; gingham ribbon; fine tip marker; light brown, medium brown and black cardstocks

Susan Merrell, Mobile, Alabama

Hail To The King

Make Dad feel like a king with this fun and regal collage. Start with a tall card base of vertically folded white cardstock. Ink entire front of card with cranberry, black and gold inks. Collage playing cards, black velveteen paper and patterned paper on card front; ink surfaces with gold ink. Adhere additional collage elements such as crown stickers, mini domino, key charm, fibers and gold "dad" tag. Cut black velveteen paper square and emboss edges with gold embossing powder; accent with gold crown embellishment, applying rhinestone jewels to crown. Apply letter stickers and stamp salutation; outline with gold pen. Punch letters from cardstock and ink with gold stamping ink. Adhere punched letters to red velveteen paper; cover with label holder and affix with brads.

Kelly Angard, Highlands Ranch, Colorado

Supplies: Patterned paper and mini domino (DMD); "dad" tag (K & Company); key charm (Magic Scraps); letter punch (Family Treasures); letter stickers (Wordsworth); letter stamps (PSX Design); rhinestones (Me & My Big Ideas); playing cards; fiber; crown stickers (source unknown); label holder (Nunn Design); red and black velveteen papers (Wintech); black, cranberry and gold stamping inks; gold embossing powder; gold pen; white cardstock

Dad

Make a Father's Day card suited for that special "king for a day." Start with a vertically-folded cream cardstock base. Ink all edges and playing cards with brown stamping ink. Dab blue stamping ink on card front. Place transparent crackle-texture sticker over face of playing card; wrap with ribbon. Mount additional playing cards facedown. Stamp sentiment onto metal-rimmed tag, cover with transparent texture sticker and attach to ribbon with tiny safety pin. Adhere to card front to complete.

Sara Horton for Tumblebeasts, Brownwood, Texas

Supplies: Transparent crackle-texture sticker (Tumblebeasts); metal-rimmed tag (Making Memories); letter stamps (PSX Design); brown, black and blue stamping inks; ribbon; safety pin; playing cards; cream cardstock

God Bless America

The embellishment on this patriotic card can be worn as jewelry. Start with a vertically folded card base of white cardstock. Cover card front with navy cardstock and accent corners with rhinestones. Stamp and emboss red cardstock with saying and adhere. Cut tag from white cardstock; trim edges in gold with leafing pen. Punch two holes in tag. To create flag, thread red, white and blue seed beads onto 13 mini safety pins. Dangle arrangement onto larger safety pin through their loops; attach large safety pin to tag.

Nancy Roth, Kittanning, Pennsylvania

Supplies: Stamp (Darcie's Country Folk); gold leafing pen (Krylon); gold stamping ink; gold embossing powder; safety pins and red, white and blue seed beads (Darice); hole punch; rhinestones; red, white and navy cardstocks

Celebrate Freedom

Create a card that's red, white and true blue. Begin with a horizontally folded white cardstock base. Tear bottom edge of card front. Adhere decorative ribbon across piece of ribbed red cardstock slightly smaller than card front; secure ends to back and tear bottom edge. Mat with navy cardstock; tear bottom edge. Write sentiment on card front with white gel pen.

Susan Merrell, Mobile, Alabama

Supplies: Flag ribbon (Offray); white gel pen; ribbed red cardstock (Bazzill); white and blue cardstocks

Stars & Stripes

Celebrate our nation's birthday with this all-American card. Begin with a horizontally folded card base of ribbed red cardstock. Cut five strips of white cardstock for flag stripes. Ink edges of card front and cardstock strips with brown stamping ink; adhere strips. Set star-shaped eyelets into textured navy cardstock rectangle; mount to upper left corner. Distress premade metal phrase and eyelets with sandpaper and adhere to card front to complete.

Melissa Lambino, West Lafayette, Indiana

Supplies: Star eyelets (Stamp Doctor); metal phrase (Making Memories); red ribbed and textured navy cardstocks (Club Scrap); brown stamping ink; sandpaper

Happy Halloween

This Halloween card employs the use of serendipity squares, which can be adapted to any theme. Begin with a card base of horizontally folded cream cardstock. Randomly stamp and emboss pumpkins with metallic green ink. For serendipity squares, tear and adhere scraps of various patterned and solid papers to completely cover a piece of cream cardstock. Stamp and emboss Halloween images over collaged paper. Free-hand create shape pattern from cardstock and use to cut out shapes from collaged paper. Mat shapes on black cardstock. Adhere gingham ribbon across front of card. Adhere serendipity squares along ribbon. Using lettering template, hand print salutation on cardstock; cut, mat with black cardstock and adhere.

MaryJo Regier, Memory Makers Books

Supplies: Patterned paper scraps (Design Originals, source unknown); lettering template (Crafter's Workshop); skeleton stamp (Rubber Stampede); large skeleton stamp (Stampendous); pumpkin stamp (PSX Design); Frankenstein stamp (Fiskars); metallic green stamping ink (Tsukineko); embossing ink; clear and black embossing powders; gingham ribbon; cream and black cardstocks

Jack-o'-lanterns

Happy jack-o'-lanterns adorn this fun Halloween card. Start with a horizontally-folded card base of speckled mustard cardstock. Tear plaid patterned paper into rough rectangle; mat with torn pumpkin patterned paper and adhere to card front. Using light box, place cream cardstock over brass stencil and dry emboss jack-o'-lanterns. Chalk embossed image using brass stencil as mask. Tear chalked image to size and adhere. Set eyelets in four corners of plaid patterned paper; thread with fibers and ribbons and tie in knots to complete.

Kari Hansen-Daffin, Memory Makers magazine

Supplies: Patterned papers (Bo-Bunny Press); brass stencil (American Traditional Designs); speckled mustard cardstock (DMD); chalk; eyelets; fibers; ribbon; cream cardstock

Homegrown

Showcase your precious harvest this Halloween. Start with vertically folded taupe cardstock for card base. Cut rectangle from textured orange cardstock; treat edges with black stamping ink and attach to card front at askew angle with brads. Adhere photo at askew angle. Affix gingham ribbon diagonally across bottom of photo. Adhere word label sticker to complete.

Mendy Douglass, Frankfort, Kentucky

Supplies: Label sticker (Pebbles); gingham ribbon (May Arts); textured orange cardstock (Bazzill); black stamping ink; black brads; photo; taupe cardstock

Supplies: Skeleton leaves, handmade paper (Nature's Handmade Paper); stamp (Stampendous); brown stamping ink; extra thick embossing powder (Suze Weinberg); metal letters (K & Company); mini brads, transparency; textured brown cardstock (Bazzill); green cardstock

Boo

Mr. Bones comes out to say "hi" on this Halloween card. Start with a vertically folded green cardstock base. Adhere skeleton leaves randomly to card front. Cut long rectangle from handmade grass paper; mat with textured brown cardstock and adhere to center. Stamp image onto transparency with brown pigment ink and emboss with clear extra thick embossing powder. Cut and attach to card front with brads. Adhere metal letters to form title.

Nicole LaCour, Memory Makers magazine

Happy Halloween

A quirky witch and candy corn make this a spooktacular Halloween card. Begin with a square card base of horizontally folded orange cardstock. Adhere pre-made photo strip across top; apply phrase sticker for sentiment. Cover remainder of card front with patterned paper. Cut stars from yellow cardstock and orange cardstocks; accent with tiny buttons, layer and adhere. Stamp saying on orange seam-binding tape; adhere at angle across bottom of card. Affix witch sticker and letter stickers to complete.

Pam Canavan, Clermont, Florida

Supplies: Patterned paper, witch sticker (Provo Craft); photo strip and ribbon (ScrapTherapy Designs); phrase sticker (EK Success); letter stickers (Me & My Big Ideas); letter stamps (PSX Design); black stamping ink; buttons; seam-binding tape; yellow and orange cardstocks

R.I.P.

Paper piece a spooky scene that folds open to reveal a Halloween message. Start with a vertically folded card base of black cardstock. Cut card front into peaked shape to resemble roof of house; cut "windows" with craft knife. Cover back of card front with yellow cardstock. Paper piece headstones from light and dark gray cardstocks. Ink edges with black stamping ink and write "R.I.P." on headstones. Paper piece pumpkins from yellow cardstock. Ink edges with orange stamping ink and add detail with orange pen. Cut stems from green cardstock; ink with green ink, add detail with pen and glue to pumpkins. Attach wire vines to pumpkin backs. Arrange paper-pieced elements and adhere. Cover interior of card with purple cardstock. Punch yellow cardstock "moon" and adhere to upper right corner of interior. Apply letter stickers for greeting.

Samantha Walker, Battle Ground, Washington

Supplies: Letter stickers (Chatterbox); circle punch (Family Treasures); black, orange and green stamping inks; wire; orange and black pens; black, yellow, light gray, dark gray and purple cardstocks

Greetings for Thanksgiving Day

Few things say Thanksgiving quite like a turkey. Begin with vertically folded square brown cardstock base. Cut slightly smaller square of patterned paper and adhere. Affix vintage-style postcard. Print quote on vellum, adhere to white cardstock and mount on bottom of postcard. Adhere leaf charms to opposite corners to complete.

Amy McGovern, Eldersburg, Maryland

Supplies: Patterned paper (source unknown); postcard (Me & My Big Ideas); leaf charms (source unknown); vellum; brown and white cardstocks

Happy Fall

Create a fall greeting collage sure to please anyone on your list. Begin with a square card base of vertically folded cream cardstock. Create background by spraying orange cardstock with walnut ink, crumpling and applying more walnut ink to creases and peaks for distressed look. Once dry, brush copper medium over surface. Cut to size and cover card front. Randomly stamp with crackle texture stamp. Cut out and tear ephemera images; apply in collage-fashion and spritz with walnut ink to age. Affix skeleton leaf and postage stamp. Die cut leaves from copper mesh; carefully heat mesh with lighter to alter color. Heat decorative copper brads in same manner. Stamp salutation on mustard cardstock. Tear piece of black cardstock and adhere to front of card near top. Layer with salutation. Affix punched mesh leaves, securing stems with mini brads. Attach decorative brads at random to complete.

Nancy Walker, Nashville, Tennessee

Supplies: Crackle rubber stamp (Nema Ink); letter stamps (Ma Vinci's); leaf die cuts (Ellison); copper mesh (AMACO); fleur de lis brads (Creative Impressions); ephemera CD (Design Originals); copper glaze (Golden Artist Colors); skeleton leaf; postage stamp; walnut ink; mini brads; brown stamping ink; mustard, black, orange and cream cardstocks

Happy Thanksgiving

Share the bounty of the season with this elegant card. Start with a vertically folded textured cream cardstock base. Cut rectangle from textured rust-colored cardstock; tear bottom edge and mount on card front. Cut patterned paper rectangle and adhere. Color metal tag and plate with copper leafing pen to change color. Attach metal plate with mini brads. Tie fiber around card crease and thread through hole in tag.

Cindy Harris, Modesto, California

Supplies: Patterned paper (Creative Imaginations); metal tag, plate and mini brads (Happy Hammer); copper leafing pen (Krylon); fiber; textured cream and rust cardstocks (Bazzill)

Supplies: Patterned papers (Me & My Big Ideas); rub-on letters (Making Memories); pre-made sticker (Westrim); sewing machine; white cardstock

Give Thanks

Create a card that looks good enough to eat! Start with a horizontally folded card base of white cardstock. Cover card front with green patterned paper. Cut two strips from contrasting patterned papers; adhere one vertically down right edge of card front and the other horizontally across bottom edge of card front. Stitch in place with sewing machine. Apply rub-on letters for sentiment. Adhere pre-made sticker to complete.

Cori Dahmen, Portland, Oregon

Happy Hanukkah

The traditional Hanukkah colors of silver and blue combined with sparkling Star of Davids create a stunning card. Begin with a long card base of horizontally folded silver cardstock. Secure ribbon across card front with brads. Affix pre-made Star of Davids on ribbon. Stamp salutation with silver ink to complete.

Kelli Noto, Centennial, Colorado

Supplies: Silver cardstock (Paper Adventures); Star of David stickers (EK Success); letter stamps (Hero Arts); ribbon (Cardeaux); silver stamping ink; brads

A Great Thing...

The look of enamel adorns this lovely Hanukkah card. Start with a vertically folded card base of textured blue cardstock. Cut rectangle from textured navy cardstock and mat with copper paper; adhere. Stamp menorah with attached sayings on white cardstock with watermark ink; emboss with blue embossing powder. Stamp identical image on dark blue cardstock with watermark ink; emboss with clear extra thick embossing powder. Paint menorah with pigment powder. Paint crescent moon on lower right of menorah; outline with pigment powder. Let dry. Apply clear lacquer over stamped image. Cut out embossed/painted menorah and mount over first menorah image. Mat assemblage with copper paper and adhere. Stamp words and emboss with copper tinsel embossing powder. Set eyelets in mat and thread with fiber to complete.

Debra Hendren, Royal Oak, Michigan

Supplies: Menorah/phrase stamp (Joan Farber); miracle stamp (Making Memories); believe stamp (Inkadinkado); watermark ink (Tsukineko); clear extra thick embossing powder (Suze Weinberg); gold, orange, silver pigment powders (USArtQuest); copper tinsel embossing powder (Stampendous); blue embossing powder; copper paper (Paper Adventures); clear lacquer; eyelets; fiber; textured navy and dark blue cardstocks (Bazzill); white cardstock

Supplies: Menorah stamp (Effie Fitzfinger); phrase stamp (PSX Design); curtain stamp (Coronado Island Stamping); glaze pens (Sakura); black and embossing inks; gold embossing powder; gold glitter glue; colored pencils; white, dark blue and speckled lavender cardstocks

Happy Hanukkah!

Placing a menorah in the window is a traditional way to start the Hanukkah season. Begin with a vertically folded white cardstock base. Stamp and emboss menorah onto dark blue cardstock. Cut slit around menorah's base. Paint candles with glazing pen and apply glitter glue to flames. Stamp window image on speckled lavender cardstock, cutting window out with a craft knife. Add detail with colored pencils. Cut stamped lavender paper and adhere, slipping window sill edge in slit in paper at menorah's base. Stamp and emboss greeting on bottom of lavender cardstock and mount.

Laurie Gore, Bonita, California

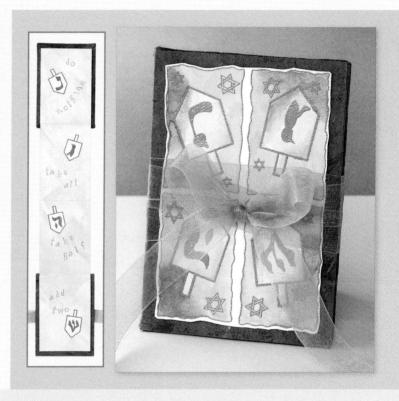

Supplies: Watercolor paper (Strathmore); navy mulberry paper (Graphic Products Corp.); dreidel stamp (Stamp Oasis); letter stamps (Hero Arts); watermark ink (Tsukineko); markers; yellow and violet stamping inks; gold embossing powder; organza ribbon; chipboard; paintbrush; plastic pallet or sheet protector; glue

Rules Of The Game

Learn how to play the ancient dreidel game with this beautiful and instructional card. Create the front and back of this fold-out card using four identical rectangles of chipboard. Cover all rectangles with navy mulberry paper and separate into pairs. Sandwich ends of ribbon lengths between two pieces of chipboard. Glue pairs of chipboard rectangles together. Let dry. Cut 30" long strip of watercolor paper that is slightly more narrow than chipboard pieces. Measure and score strip every 5" and accordion-fold into six equal sections. Ink front of entire strip with yellow stamping ink. On separate piece of watercolor paper, use watermark ink to stamp dreidel images in mosaic-pattern of four. Stamp four additional dreidels to cut out. Heat emboss all images with gold embossing powder. Silhouette-cut four individual dreidels and adhere to sections 2-4 of long yellow strip. Stamp instructions on each section of yellow strip. Glue front of sections 1 and 6 to back side of chipboard front and back. Create the look of watercolor paint on the stamped images by scribbling marker on a plastic paint pallet (or sheet protector) and adding a drop or two of water to dilute. Apply to stamped image using watercolor brush. Let paper dry completely; cut out and adhere to card front. Apply additional marker "paint" to a blank watercolor paper rectangle. Once dry, stamp sentiment with letter stamps and adhere to back of card. Secure closed by wrapping with ribbon and tying into bow.

Laurie Gore, Bonita, California

Happy Chanukah

Celebrate special elements and traditions of Hanukkah such as the dreidel. Start with a card base of vertically folded textured lavender cardstock. Attach patterned paper to card front with decorative eyelets. Die-cut letters for sentiment and dreidel from watercolor paper. Detail letters and dreidel with chalk pencils, paint with shimmer paint and adhere. Affix dreidel to textured lavender cardstock rectangle and ink edges with purple ink; mount to finish.

Kathi Rerek, Scotch Plains, New Jersey

Supplies: Patterned paper (Sandylion); dreidel and letters (QuicKutz); Star of David eyelets (source unknown); watercolor paper (Canson); pigment paint (Angelwings Enterprises); chalk pencils (Derwent); textured lavender cardstock (Bazzill)

Celebrate The Miracle...

Several shapes and strategic use of embossing combine to form this elaborate menorah. Start with a horizontally folded blue cardstock base. For menorah components, cut a long strip and punch nine squares and two triangles from cardstock; cut hexagon in half to create base and layer triangles to form Star of David. Construct menorah by gluing star in center of strip on cut hexagon and square "candle holders" along strip and atop star. Once completely dry, run facedown through adhesive application machine. Coat sticker surface with brass embossing powder; heat set. Immediately emboss a second application; accent with rhinestones. For candles, die cut from cardstock scraps; cut off "flames," ink with watermark pad and heat set with clear embossing powder. Die cut nine more from white watercolor paper and utilize flames only; paint with watercolors and allow to dry. Coat with crystal lacquer and let set. Glue candles into "holders," run assemblage through adhesive application machine and apply to card base. Glue flames into place. For greeting, die cut letters, run through adhesive machine and heat emboss with brass powder.

Kathi Rerek, Scotch Plains, New Jersey

Supplies: Hexagon punch (Emagination Crafts); square punch (EK Success); triangle, candle, letters (QuicKutz); watermark ink (Tsukineko); clear and gold embossing powder; adhesive application machine (Xyron); pigment paint (Angelwings Enterprises); rhinestones; clear lacquer; gold cardstock (Club Scrap); watercolor paper (Canson); bright blue cardstock, multiple colored scraps of cardstock

Kwanzaa

Eight candles in the bright colors of Kwanzaa grace this card. Begin with a long horizontally folded card base of sand cardstock. Treat edges of torn taupe cardstock strip with black stamping ink. Create candles with red, yellow and green acrylic paints; outline with black pen. Hand draw flames. Ink edges of card front with brown stamping ink. Poke two holes in fold of card; accent with colorful fibers. Affix letter stickers along bottom of card front. Apply glitter glue to candle flames and around edges to finish.

Erikia Ghumm, Brighton, Colorado

Supplies: Letter stickers (K & Company); red, green and yellow acrylic paints; black pen; glitter glue; brown and black stamping inks; fibers; taupe and sand cardstocks

Supplies: Background stamp (Clearsnap); animal stamps (Stampin' Up!); watermark pen (Tsuki-neko); letter stickers (Wordsworth); beads (Blue Moon Beads); bamboo clips (7 Gypsies); skeleton leaves (Nature's Handmade Paper); fibers; black, red and green cardstocks; gold pigment powder; black and gold stamping inks

Kwanzaa

Honor Kwanzaa with rich and beautiful accents for an exquisite card. Begin with a horizontally folded black cardstock base. Cover entire card with red cardstock, leaving one-quarter inch of black cardstock showing on bottom edge of card front. Layer with green cardstock, leaving one-quarter inch of red cardstock showing along bottom edge of card front and approximately 1½" of red showing on left side of card front. Stamp background image onto green cardstock with black ink. Using craft knife, cut away sections of card in layers to mimic background stamp. Stamp animal images on card front and interior; dust with gold pigment powder. Dab skeleton leaf with gold stamping ink. Cut rectangular piece from card front in upper right corner to reveal portion of interior. Outline elements of card with watermark pen; dust with gold pigment powder. Attach fibers with bamboo clips. Double mat letter stickers on jagged-cut green cardstock; add color with watermark pen, dust with gold pigment powder and attach with foam spacers. Adhere beads across bottom to represent candles. For flames, draw with watermark pen and emboss with gold embossing powder.

Andrea Lyn Vetten-Marley, Aurora, Colorado

Joy, Hope, Peace, Faith

Words of the season adorn this elegant card. Start with a horizontally folded metallic red cardstock base. Glue strip of striped gold paper to bottom edge of card; add gold cord along seam. Stamp and emboss four phrases onto silver cardstock; cut into tag shapes, punch holes in tops and tear bottom edges. Apply gold leafing pen to torn edge, color with watermark pen and rub with gold metallic pigment powder. Tie tags with fiber. Affix holly stickers; glue on rhinestone "berries." Adhere tags to card front.

Shawna Rendon, Memory Makers magazine

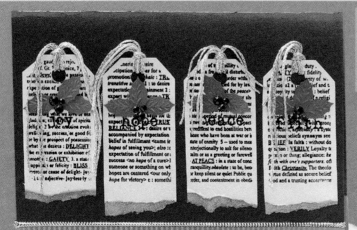

Supplies: Phrase stamps (My Sentiments Exactly); gold leafing pen (Krylon); 3-D holly stickers (EK Success); metallic red and silver cardstocks (Paper Illuzionz); watermark pen (Tsukineko); fibers (Fiber Scraps, Timeless Touches); gold card (Cardeaux); gold pigment powder; black stamping ink; clear embossing powder; rhinestones; fiber; gold stripe

Supplies: Rub on word, phrase, charm (Making Memories); textured red, green and light green cardstocks (Bazzill); ribbon

Supplies: Laminate chip (Lowe's); letter stickers (EK Success); gingham ribbon, brads; red stamping ink; textured white and green cardstocks (Bazzill)

The Magic Of Christmas

Clean, graphic lines create an attractive, simply stated card. Start with a horizontally folded textured red cardstock base. Adhere strip of textured green cardstock across card front. Adhere thin strip of textured light green cardstock below. Hang ornament charm on ribbon, securing ends to back of card flap. Rub on sentiment to complete.

Sara Graham, Orlando, Florida

Ho Ho Ho

Here a dressed-up laminate chip makes for a charming accent. Begin with a tall vertically folded white textured cardstock base. Treat card edges with red stamping ink. Apply letter stickers to laminate chip and tie gingham ribbon through hole. Attach strip of textured green cardstock with brads to hold tag.

Emily Garza, Layton, Utah

Merry Christmas

This clever tree is quick to create. Begin with a vertically folded textured red cardstock base. Cut rectangle from textured tan cardstock.
Cut elongated triangle from textured dark green cardstock; section
diagonally. Adhere strip of textured brown cardstock down center of
tan rectangle. Set eyelets on tree sections and adhere, leaving space between. Mat tan rectangle on dark green cardstock; mount to card front.
Adhere metal title charm and accent tree with star brad.

Julie Day, Meaghers Grant, Nova Scotia, Canada

*Supplies: Phrase charm, star brad (Making
Memories); eyelets; textured red, green, tan
and brown cardstocks (Bazzill)*

Love, Trust, Joy...

Traditional Christmas colors and patterns combine to make this lovely card. Begin with a vertically folded green
cardstock base. Tear vintage holly-patterned paper into rectangle and mount. Cover large pre-made slide mount
with contrasting holly paper and accent with gingham ribbon. Stamp sentiment onto red cardstock; emboss with
black embossing powder. Frame stamped cardstock with slide mount. Using decorative scissors, trim red cardstock
around slide mount. Embellish with woven tag and threaded button; adhere.

Kari Hansen-Daffin, Memory Makers magazine

*Supplies: Patterned papers (Anna Griffin); large slide mount (Foofala); word stamp (My Sentiments
Exactly); woven label (Me & My Big Ideas); clear embossing powder; black stamping ink; button;
gingham ribbon; green and red cardstocks*

Season's Greetings

Here the art of iris folding creates a beautifully artistic yuletide tree. Start with a vertically-folded base of cream cardstock. See instructions below to create iris-folding element. Once assemblage is complete, punch tiny holes near points of tree branches and weave gold thread through holes in crisscross pattern over tree opening. Adhere to card front. Stamp greeting onto cream cardstock and emboss with topiary-colored embossing powder. Ink edges of greeting with gold and dark green inks; adhere. Affix star rhinestone to top of tree.

Nancy Walker, Nashville, Tennessee

Supplies: Patterned papers (Brother Sister Design Studio, Frances Meyer, Hot Off The Press); tree die cut (Sizzix); stamp (Close To My Heart); green and gold stamping inks; topiary embossing powder (PSX Design), star rhinestone (Buttons Galore); gold paper (source unknown); gold thread; green and cream cardstocks

1 Cut rectangle from green paper; die cut tree in center. Cut two ¾" strips from three coordinating patterned papers; cut each in half. Score ¼" from bottom of each strip and fold.

3 Collect cut strips by print pattern and assign each grouping a letter, A, B or C. Layer strips according to letter designated, starting with 1A, then 2A, and so forth, progressing along each side of die cut shape and trimming pieces as needed. Continue layering strips over pattern until shape is filled.

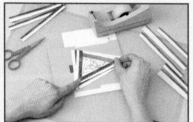

2 Using temporary adhesive, tape pattern provided on page 125 to work mat. Center rectangle over tree pattern front-side-down. Add small brown cardstock piece to fill trunk of tree.

4 Remove assemblage from pattern; flip over and adhere small piece of holographic paper to back of assemblage to show through tree center.

...Days 'Til Christmas

Countdown the days until Christmas using the spinning feature on this clever card. Begin with a vertically folded white cardstock base. Cover front of card with patterned paper. Tint photo elements using editing software or with tinting pens; mat on textured red cardstock. Treat edges of red mat with black stamping ink; adhere photo. Stamp countdown phrase onto textured red cardstock; ink edges and adhere to card front. Cut out window through all layers of card front, just to the left of phrase. Cut white cardstock circle, write numbers around edge and ink edge of circle. Punch small hole in center of circle. Position so numbers show through window. Fasten number wheel to back of card front with decorative brad; leaving just a bit showing beyond card edge for turning.

Natalie Quandt, Rochester, Minnesota

Supplies: Patterned paper (7 Gyspies); snowflake brad (Creative Impressions); letter stamps (PSX Design); black stamping ink; textured red cardstock (Bazzill); black pen; white cardstock

Wishing You Joy

Look closely and you'll see a fun way to spell out "joy" for your annual holiday card. Begin by vertically folding a white cardstock base. Layer card front with textured light blue and torn navy blue cardstocks. Using a variety of computer fonts, print sentiment onto white cardstock, leaving room for photos. Photograph volunteer human "letters" to form portion of sentiment. Mat photo with navy cardstock, adhere to printed sentiment and apply metallic rub-ons to torn edge. Mount assembly to card front. Tie fibers through charm and mount on torn navy cardstock square. Adhere to left lower corner of card front. Stamp date in lower right corner and heat emboss with white embossing powder to complete.

Melanie Bruner, Knoxville, Tennessee

Supplies: Date stamp and ornament charm (Making Memories); textured light blue and navy cardstocks (Bazzill); fiber; white embossing powder; pigment stamping ink; metallic rub-ons; white cardstock

Season's Greetings

Cool, frosty colors create an elegant look for this holiday card. Begin with a card base of horizontally folded white cardstock. Stamp sentiment repeatedly on sea foam-colored cardstock; emboss with white powder. Cut and adhere to top half of card front. Stamp bottom half of card front repeatedly with sea foam ink; emboss with clear embossing powder. Create square embellishment with white and sea foam rectangles; affix thin strips of double-sided tape around edges. Apply silver metal flakes to tape. Punch three leaves from white cardstock; run through adhesive application machine. Apply silver metal flakes to punched leaves and adhere. Apply sea foam green ink to brads and emboss with clear embossing powder. Fasten to center of card to complete.

MaryJo Regier, Memory Makers Books

Supplies: Phrase stamp (My Sentiments Exactly); metal flake (Biblical Impressions); holly punch (Emagination Crafts); sea foam green and stamping inks; white and clear embossing powders; brads; tacky tape; sea foam green and white cardstocks

Joy

Stamped velvet adds soft dimension to this holiday card. Start with a horizontally folded rust cardstock base. Cut long rectangle of brown cardstock; punch top corners with corner punch. Apply title using lettering template and copper leafing pen. Tear bottom from brown cardstock, coat torn edge with glue and emboss with copper embossing powder. For velvet pieces, choose larger images. Place rubber stamp rubber-side-up on ironing board. Cover stamp with heavy upholstery velvet nap-side-down against stamp. Set iron on cotton setting. Spritz back of velvet with water and press hot iron onto velvet over stamp. With moderate pressure, hold iron in place for 10-20 seconds. Lift off velvet to reveal stamped image. For pine cones, ink stamp first with black dye stamping ink; repeat ironing technique and cut pieces to size. Apply glue to edges of pine bough element and heat emboss with copper embossing powder. Slip corners of pine bough element under punched corners of brown cardstock. Affix cardstock to card front with brads. Fasten ribbon down left side of card. Adhere pine cone pieces to ribbon.

Torrey Miller, Thornton, Colorado

Supplies: Brown and green velvet (Jo-Ann Fabric); lettering template (Scrap Pagerz); gold leafing pen (Krylon); corner punch (EK Success); pinecone and bough stamps (Stampin' Up!); black stamping ink; glue; copper embossing powder; mini brads; ribbon; rust and brown cardstocks

You've Been Mistle-Toad

Share a tongue-in-cheek holiday greeting with those you love! Begin with a horizontally folded red cardstock base. Layer with sections of torn patterned paper and white handmade paper; accent with decorative brads. For tag element, stamp image onto back of acrylic tag with black solvent-based ink. Color with pigment pen and set with heat gun. Apply glue and sprinkle on glitter. Let dry. Tie tag with fibers and adhere. Apply letter stickers to card front for first portion of title and die cut letters for remainder. Tie sparkle fiber across top and affix mistletoe sticker to complete.

Jodi Amidei, Memory Makers Books

Supplies: *Acrylic tag (Sunday International); frog stamp (Biblical Impressions); black solvent ink (Tsukineko); mistletoe sticker (EK Success); die-cut letters (QuicKutz); letter stickers (Wordsworth); patterned paper (Carolee's Creations); glitter (Magic Scraps); white handmade paper (Nature's Handmade Paper); star brads (Creative Impressions); red pigment pen; glue; fibers; red cardstock*

Dear Santa

Bring back the nostalgia of writing letters to Saint Nick. Begin with a card base of horizontally folded cream cardstock. Cut patterned paper rectangle and mat with rust cardstock; mount. Stamp premade packing tag with text stamp. Tie tag with gingham ribbon and adhere diagonally to card front. Adhere die-cut letters on tag for title. Santa image was downloaded from the Internet, printed and matted with rust cardstock. Adhere to card to complete.

Ellen Bentley-Fikes, Glenburn, Maine

Supplies: *Patterned paper (DMD); die-cut letters (QuicKutz); text stamp (Hero Arts); tag (Magic Scraps); brown stamping ink; gingham ribbon; Santa clip art; cream and rust cardstocks*

Birthdays

chapter 2

Celebrate

This happy card can be made in any monochromatic color scheme. Start with horizontally folded textured lavender cardstock base. Cut strips of textured purple and plum cardstocks and adhere side by side across card front. Die cut balloons from lilac and lavender textured cardstocks; assemble, wrap with purple wire around ends and adhere. Attach thin strip of textured lavender cardstock across card front and bend balloon "strings" around strip. Secure strip to card front with lavender snaps. Apply letter stickers for greeting.

Julie Day, Meaghers Grant, Nova Scotia, Canada

Supplies: Letter stickers (Doodlebug Design); balloon die cuts (Ellison); purple wire; snaps (Making Memories); lavender, lilac, plum and purple textured cardstocks (Bazzill)

Happy Birthday To You

This colorful card's pre-made library pocket can hold a tag or small gift. Begin with a vertically folded card base of light green paper; cover card front with striped patterned paper. Adhere pre-made library pocket. Cut thin strips of coordinating patterned paper and adhere at askew angle to pocket front. Cut tag shape from dot-patterned paper; punch hole and thread gingham ribbon through. Apply letter stickers to pocket front for greeting. Adhere sticker to tag for sentiment. Detail card, tag and pocket with black pen.

Tracy Miller, Fallston, Maryland

Supplies: Patterned papers (SEI); library pocket (Li'l Davis Designs); letter and sentiment stickers (Wordsworth); gingham ribbon (Making Memories); hole punch; black pen

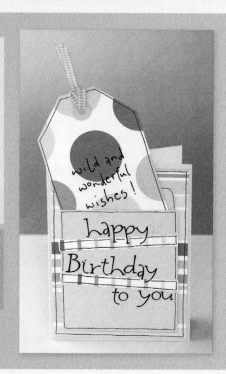

Supplies: Light blue, lime green, purple, yellow, and hot pink speckled cardstocks and acrylic token (Doodlebug Design); flower punch (All Night Media); colored and flower brads (Provo Craft); flower buttons (Making Memories); flower appliqué (Marcel Schurman); printed vellum (source unknown); ribbon; floss; textured light pink and dark pink cardstocks (Bazzill)

1,2,3...

Create a card that's fun and educational for a favorite little girl. Begin with a horizontally folded textured pink cardstock base; tear bottom edge from card front. Adhere thin strips of textured dark pink cardstock across card front to form five sections. Adhere torn section of printed vellum to lower left section. Die cut numbers and sentiment from brightly colored speckled cardstock; affix to individual sections in numeric order. Embellish sections with ribbon-tied acrylic token, flower appliqué, floss-threaded flower-shaped buttons, punched flowers with brad centers and colored flower brads in quantities specific to respective section.

Janet Miller, Northeast, Pennsylvania

4th Birthday

This brightly colored card can be adapted to any age by simply changing the number and greeting. Begin with a vertically folded card base of white cardstock. Cover front with patterned vellum; secure with colored brads in corners. Paint house number from hardware store with red acrylic paint; let dry and adhere to card front. Secure punch-label greetings to card front with color-coordinated brads.

Shannon Taylor, Bristol, Tennessee

Supplies: Patterned vellum (Creative Imaginations); house number (Hy-Ko Products); punch labels (Dymo); colored brads (Karen Foster Design); red acrylic paint; white cardstock

Undeniable Proof

The evidence is irrefutable that this is one clever birthday card. Begin with a pre made mini file folder. Accent with ledger patterned paper and sections from printed transparency. Alter black-and-white photos in photo editing software program to "tint"; print photos on white cardstock, cut into strips and adhere to card front and interior. Print title and sentiments on regular printer paper; cut to size, ink edges with black stamping ink and adhere at random to card front and interior. Affix magnifying glass to frame photo on card front. Attach paper clip to top of card and add real fingerprints throughout card to complete.

Carrie O'Donnell, Newburyport, Massachusetts

Supplies: Mini file folder (Rusty Pickle); patterned paper (Making Memories); printed transparency (7 Gypsies); magnifying glass (www.mantofev.com); envelope (www.absolutelyeverything.com); red permanent marker; black stamping ink; paper clip; white cardstock

Toot Toot! You're 3

This unassuming birthday card opens up to reveal a treasure trove any toddler would love! The base is a coin-holder book which can be purchased at coin or hobby shops. Paint book's interior with white acrylic paint; let dry. Coat with black acrylic paint. When dry, distress using sandpaper in circular motions. Cover outside of coin book with blue cardstock. Ink all edges with black ink. Adhere train sticker along bottom edge of card front, continuing on to card back. Write title on light blue cardstock tag; punch hole, insert silver brad and mount. Apply number sticker. Place photo on card front to complete card's exterior. On interior, decorate each compartment with a variety of found objects, coins, foil-wrapped chocolates, punched brass foil shapes and rhinestones. Create sentiments using label maker to finish.

Susan Cyrus, Broken Arrow, Oklahoma

Supplies: Train sticker (Tumblebeasts); hand, dragonfly and frog punches (McGill); decorative buttons (Jesse James); typewriter cut-out word (DMD); number sticker (Creative Imaginations); punch labels (Dymo); fork charm (EK Success); chocolates; black stamping ink; rhinestones; coins; brass foil; blue, white and yellow cardstocks

Hauling in Loads...

This card brings on the big rigs to deliver truckloads of birthday joy. Begin with a horizontally folded card base of blue cardstock; ink with black stamping ink. Ink edges of red and yellow cardstock rectangles with black ink; mount and adhere. Apply stickers to white cardstock; cut out and mount with foam adhesive. Use label maker to create salutation; cut apart and adhere. Cover metal washers with embossing ink and heat emboss with several layers of black extra thick embossing powder. Adhere embossed washers to card front.

Denise Tucker, Versailles, Indiana

Supplies: Truck stickers (Tumblebeasts); label maker (Dymo); black extra thick embossing powder (Ranger); washers; black and embossing inks; foam spacers; red, white, bright blue and yellow cardstocks

Wish

Send birthday wishes with this beautiful card. Start with horizontally folded square purple cardstock base. Tear and adhere patterned paper square to card front; apply decoupage adhesive along lower edge. Press and crumple strip of torn patterned tissue paper into adhesive; let dry. Adhere beaded dragonfly stickers. Affix snap letters above tissue paper strip. Punch two holes along card's crease; thread with ribbon and tie into bow.

Kari Hansen-Daffin, Memory Makers magazine

Supplies: Patterned paper (Karen Foster Design); patterned tissue (DMD); snap letters (All My Memories); dragonfly stickers (EK Success); hole punch; ribbon; purple cardstock

Pocket Paper Doll

Here's a fun gift card for any little girl. Start with a vertically folded cream cardstock base. Layer with coordinating patterned papers. Cover and line library pocket with patterned paper; adhere pink ribbon and mount. Stamp doll and clothes on white cardstock. Color with colored pencils, cut out and slip into pocket. Cut two slits with craft knife at top of card; thread with ribbon and tie into bow.

Emily Curry Hitchingham, Memory Makers Books

Supplies: Patterned papers (Me & My Big Ideas); library pockets (Anima Designs); paper doll/clothes stamps (Holly Berry House); dragonfly punch (EK Success); ribbon (Anna Griffin); colored pencils; cream cardstock

Happy Birthday To You

Make creative use of all those free software CDs you receive in the mail. Start with a square card base of horizontally folded orange cardstock; cover with patterned transparency. Using a word processing program, create sentiment using "Word Art" feature; print on transparency. Trace around CD with a grease pencil onto printed transparency; cut to size. Iron HeatnBond to wrong side of floral fabric according to manufacturer directions; cut out flower. Adhere CD to card front; cover with transparency and place flower on top. Secure all to card front with brad.

Diana Hudson, Bakersfield, California

Supplies: Patterned transparency (Magic Scraps); transparency (3M); CD; floral fabric; mini brad; orange cardstock

Supplies: Patterned papers (Lasting Impressions); tag (Westrim); letter stamps (PSX Design); charm (www.maudeandmillie.com); organza ribbon

Happy Birthday

Here's a card that's all wrapped up and waiting to be opened. Begin with a horizontally folded striped lavender base. Cut rectangle from yellow patterned paper. Cut strip of coordinating yellow paper and adhere to top of rectangle to create "package." Tie bow, securing pre-made tag in knot. Stamp salutation on tag with black ink. Adhere charm tied with tiny bow to tag front.

Polly McMillan, Bullhead City, Arizona

Birthday Kimono

A pretty kimono shape comprises this unique card. Cover interior with green patterned paper. Stamp front with Asian character stamp using purple and lime green inks and lanterns with black ink. Fill in background and add detail to lanterns with watercolor paints. Write sentiments with purple and lavender markers. Punch two holes through card on both sides of "bodice." Thread with cording and accent with Asian coin.

Kari Hansen-Daffin, Memory Makers magazine

Supplies: Kimono card (Stampendous); green patterned paper (Making Memories); Asian character stamp (PSX Design); lantern stamp (Rubber Stampede); paper cord (Yasutomo); coin (Boxer Scrapbook Productions); watercolors; lime green, black and purple stamping inks; purple and lavender markers

Rootin' Tootin' Birthday Boy

This card is perfect for any cowpoke. Start with a long card base of horizontally folded western patterned paper. See instructions to follow for clay photo transfer element. Cut strip of red bandanna paper; mat with book page patterned paper and adhere to card front along bottom. Mat clay transfer element with handmade grass paper; affix diagonally to card front with star brads. Apply letter stickers to handmade grass paper strips for title; secure to card front with star brads. Adhere toy sheriff's badge to upper right corner. Make a lasso from paper cording and adhere to complete.

Torrey Miller, Thornton, Colorado

Supplies: Western patterned papers (K & Company); book page paper (DMD); polymer clay (Polyform Products); letter stickers (Wordsworth); handmade grass paper (Nature's Handmade Paper); star brads (Magic Scraps); paper cord; color photocopy; toy badge

1 Duplicate photo three times on regular copy paper. Cut and tape together in photo-strip formation. Roll out polymer clay into ¼" thickness. Layer with photo strip image-side-down; spritz with water. Press photo strip into clay with small rolling pin.

2 Using a craft knife, trim photo strip along edges. Bake according to manufacturer instructions, leaving photo strip on clay piece.

3 Allow to cool completely. Spritz photo strip with water; remove from clay by gently peeling and rolling with finger to reveal image.

A Very Happy Birthday

Bring back the "mod" look with this groovy birthday card. Start off with a horizontally folded glossy white cardstock base. Cover card front with party napkin. Adhere glossy white cardstock rectangle to card front. In a well-ventilated area, spray various colors of stained-glass paint onto transparency according to manufacturer directions; allow to dry. Punch several various-sized circles from painted transparency. Stamp birthday words on reverse side of two of the circles with solvent-based ink. Arrange circles on card front and adhere. Stamp greeting on non-painted side of transparency; mount on white cardstock and die-cut into tag shape. Thread leather cord through hole and adhere with foam spacers.

Kelli Noto, Centennial, Colorado

Supplies: Stained-glass paint (Krylon); sentiment stamp (My Sentiments Exactly); greeting stamp (Anna Griffin); black solvent ink (Tsukineko); tag die (Sizzix); circle punches (Family Treasures); leather cord (Hot Off The Press); party napkin (American Greetings); transparency; foam spacers; glossy white cardstock

You Rock

Tell that special teen just how you feel in terms he or she will understand with this edgy birthday card. Vertically fold a long rectangle from white cardstock to form base. Cover card front with patterned transparency. Adhere letter stickers to metal-rimmed tags for sentiment and affix to card front with foam adhesive. Mount guitar die cut to card and finish with label maker sentiment.

Kelli Noto, Centennial Colorado

Supplies: Patterned transparency (Magic Scraps); metal-rimmed tags, tag stickers (EK Success); guitar die cut (Paper House Productions); label maker (Dymo); foam adhesive; white cardstock

Guess Who's Turning One?

Celebrate your baby's milestone birthday in style with this personalized invitation. Start with a horizontally folded card base of textured brown cardstock. Adhere blue cardstock and photo to card front. Cut brown cardstock strip and affix to card across bottom of photo with brads. Print title and invitation details on blue cardstock; cut to size. Apply typewriter sticker to strip. In card's interior, mount blue cardstock invitation details.

Emily Garza, Layton, Utah

Supplies: Stickers (EK Success); textured brown cardstock (Bazzill); mini brads; photo; blue cardstock

Mall Madness

Decorate a pre-made mini gift bag for a quick, fun party invitation. Start by printing title on white cardstock; cut to size and mat with ribbed light blue cardstock. Apply shoe sticker and tiny price tag to torn blue mulberry paper; adhere to title block and mount to bag. Design invitation to look like gift certificate using desktop publishing software; print on regular printer paper. Fill bag with tissue paper and partially slide "gift certificate" into bag.

Annette Gulati, Round Rock, Texas

Supplies: Mini gift bag (Hobby Lobby); shoe sticker (Colorbök); mini tag (DMD); textured light blue cardstock (Bazzill); black pen; tissue paper; printer paper; blue mulberry paper; white cardstock

Amanda & Daniel

Create a unique and elegant party invitation with a long tag tucked into a vellum sleeve. Print party details on a long piece of white cardstock. Stamp castle image on invitation with rainbow ink; emboss with glitter embossing powder. Cut invitation to size and adhere to long strip of light green cardstock. Apply glue along edge of invitation and sprinkle with green glitter. Punch hole in top of invitation and tie with organza ribbon. Print guests' names on vellum; outline with glue and coat with green glitter. Construct tall sleeve from printed vellum. Slide invitation inside to complete.

Cheryl Uribe, Grapevine, Texas

Supplies: Castle stamp (source unknown); rainbow stamping ink; glitter embossing powder; organza ribbon; glue; green glitter; vellum; white and light green cardstocks

You're Invited...

Use a real zipper to create charming slumber party invitations. Start with a vertically folded card base of textured pink cardstock. Cover card front with polka-dot patterned paper. Add a triangle of coordinating polka-dot paper to bottom right corner, adhering only tall side and bottom edge to form a pocket. Apply tacky tape to zipper's fabric; unzip and adhere along left side of card and seam of pocket. Using a template, cut small and large tags from light pink cardstock. Mount polka-dot paper to small tag and brown dotted paper to large tag. Print salutations on vellum; cut into respective tag shapes and affix over tags with eyelets. Tie organza ribbon on large tag and slip into zipper pocket. Adhere small tag over pocket.

Lisa Dixon, East Brunswick, New Jersey

Supplies: Patterned papers (KI Memories); zipper (Coats & Clark); tag template (Provo Craft); organza ribbon (May Arts); textured light pink and darker pink cardstocks (Bazzill); eyelets; tacky tape

Zoom On Over...

What little birthday boy or girl wouldn't love an animal safari party? In word processing program, create wrap-around text for card front by manipulating text within a text box. Print on red cardstock. Collage card front with corrugated paper, patterned paper and textured zebra fabric; treat with black stamping ink. Print title onto sand cardstock and tear out; stamp with zebra stamp and ink torn edges with black ink. Affix to black cardstock with eyelets at askew angle. Stamp party details on patterned paper; cut into square, ink edges with brown stamping ink and adhere to back side of card.

Samantha Walker, Battle Ground, Washington

Supplies: Patterned papers (Chatterbox); corrugated paper, zebra fabric (Flax Art & Design); letter and zebra stamps (Stampin' Up!); eyelets; black and brown stamping inks; black, red and sand cardstocks

Looks Like A Party For...

Create a party invitation for your favorite little superhero. Start with a horizontally folded red cardstock card base. Print greeting on blue cardstock; cut and mount on card front. Apply sticker to white cardstock and silhouette; mount with foam spacers. Print party details on yellow cardstock; cut and mount on card's interior with logo sticker.

Leah Blanco Williams, Kansas City, Missouri

Supplies: Superman stickers (Creative Imaginations); foam spacers; yellow, red and bright blue cardstocks

1950

Hearken back to the year of the birthday person's birth with a baby photo and era-specific patterned papers. Start with a horizontally folded textured pink cardstock base. Cover with retro patterned paper. Apply strip of diamond-patterned paper along left edge. Stamp and emboss retro clock image randomly onto card front. Cut window in upper right corner of card front to create photo frame. Slide photocopy of photo between patterned paper and cardstock, adhering to backside of cardstock flap. Cover card interior with patterned paper. Punch tiny diamonds from pink cardstock and adhere around window opening. Die cut birth year from green cardstock and adhere.

Emily Curry Hitchingham, Memory Makers Books

Supplies: Patterned papers (SEI); clock stamp (Paper Candy); die-cut numbers (QuicKutz); embossing ink; white embossing powder; diamond punch (Emagination Crafts); letter stickers (Karen Foster Design); textured pink cardstock (Bazzill); copied photo

Happy Birthday

Bold strips in bright colors make this birthday card sing! Start with a horizontally folded card base of peach cardstock. Layer with pink cardstock. Cut strips of cardstock in dark pink, purple, lavender and orange. Horizontally adhere strips; accent corner with metal plaque embellishment. Print title onto white cardstock; mat with peach cardstock and treat edges with dark brown ink. Adhere to card front to complete.

Melissa Lambino, West Lafayette, Indiana

Supplies: Metal plaque (Making Memories); peach, pink, dark pink, purple, lavender and orange textured cardstocks (Bazzill); stamping ink; white cardstock

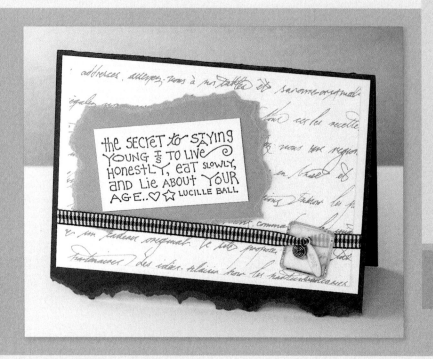

The Secret To Staying Young...

Create an elegant birthday card that any adult will cherish. Start with a card base of horizontally-folded dark brown cardstock. Tear off bottom edge. Cut rectangle from patterned paper; mat with cream cardstock and mount on card front. Stamp sentiment on cream cardstock with black ink; mount on torn piece of tan cardstock and adhere. Thread metal-rimmed tag, charm and metal date tag onto gingham ribbon and adhere across card to complete.

Stephanie Mosher, Kyle, Texas

Supplies: Patterned paper (7 Gypsies); quote stamp (Paula Best); black stamping ink; metal date tag (Making Memories); spiral charm (source unknown); gingham ribbon; metal-rimmed tag; cream, tan and dark brown cardstocks

You've Come A Long Way Baby

Here's a fun peekaboo birthday card sure to cheer anyone on your birthday list. Use a premade mosaic-style window card base, or cut your own windows in white cardstock with a craft knife. Treat card front with dark moss, olive, yellow ochre and amber clay stamping inks, starting with darkest color first. Choose one color and repeat on inside of card. Cut or punch vintage images to be framed by windows; adhere to inside of card. Print sentiment onto transparency; attach to card with decorative brads.

Jodi Amidei, Memory Makers Books

Supplies: Pre-made window card (DMD); dark moss, olive, yellow ochre and amber clay stamping inks (Clearsnap); copper brads (Creative Impressions); transparency; vintage magazine images

Birthday

Maximize space and incorporate many patterns using a template. Start with a horizontally folded white cardstock card base. Adorn card front with strips, rectangles and squares of patterned paper, mustard corrugated paper and rust cardstock. Arrange and adhere paper to form mosaiclike background. Thread turquoise beads onto copper floss and tie across top of card. Stamp birthday definition onto vellum; cut out and secure to card with copper brads. Punch shapes from copper sheet and adhere to card to complete.

Candice Cruz, Somerville, Massachusetts

Supplies: Card template (Deluxe Designs); patterned paper (KI Memories); shape punch (EK Success); copper sheet (AMACO); copper floss (DMC); birthday stamp (Hero Arts); stamping ink; mini copper brads; beads; vellum; mustard corrugated paper; white and rust cardstocks.

Happy Birthday

A little ink and paper tearing easily add artistic flair. This postcard-style birthday wish begins with a green patterned paper base. Mount blue patterned paper section to card front. Tear strips of striped and text-patterned papers; adhere. Create envelope from green patterned paper and mount. Print messages on rust patterned paper. Stamp sentiment on twill tape and treat with ink. Randomly ink entire card with black ink. Set rivets along top left of card. Create spiral wire "clip" and use to secure twill word and torn patterned paper to envelope. Insert message into envelope. Adhere twill ribbon along right edge of card to finish.

Brooke Campbell, Shelley, Idaho

Supplies: Blue and striped patterned papers and rivets (Chatterbox); text-patterned paper (Colorbök); alphabet stamps (Hero Arts); black stamping ink; twill tape; wire

Happy Birthday

A vintage accent and a modern office supply element blend beautifully to create this birthday card. Start with a vertically folded burgundy cardstock card base. Mount diamond-print paper to card front. Layer with floral motif paper at askew angle. Overlap with pre-made ephemera tag. Finish with a label tape title.

Tracy Miller, Fallston, Maryland

Supplies: Patterned paper (L'il Davis Designs); floral paper (DMD); ephemera tag (Me & My Big Ideas); label tape (Dymo); burgundy cardstock

Supplies: Patterned papers (Anna Griffin); textured cream cardstock (Bazzill); brown stamping ink; metal-rimmed tag; ribbon

Happy Birthday

Botanical patterned paper of a vintage feel adds an air of sophistication to this lovely card. Start with a vertically folded card base of textured cream cardstock. Treat edges of patterned paper with brown stamping ink; adhere to card front. Print sentiment onto patterned paper; cut into circle, ink and mount inside metal-rimmed tag. Set eyelet in tag; tie ribbon around card and through tag to complete.

Janet Hopkins, Frisco, Texas

Make A Wish

Candles aren't the only things you blow on to make a wish. Create beautiful hand-stitched dandelions to help extend birthday wishes. Start with a vertically folded textured dark green cardstock base. See instructions below for hand-stitched flowers. Stamp sentiment on mustard cardstock with brown stamping ink; tear to size and affix with brads. Mat on gold cardstock. Tear rough rectangle from mustard cardstock. With sewing machine, stitch to card front. Adhere dandelion assemblage to complete.

Kelly Angard, Highlands Ranch, Colorado

Supplies: Letter stamps (PSX Design); brown stamping ink; mini brads; embroidery floss (DMC); textured dark green cardstock (Bazzill); mustard and green cardstocks

1 On a mouse pad, use an anywhere punch to punch two small holes to serve as flower centers. Freehand pierce dandelion in green paper rectangle.

2 Using three colors of embroidery floss, hand stitch stems and petals using chain, straight stitches and French knots, respectively.

Golden Birthday

A collage is a beautiful way to send a special friend a joyous birthday wish. Start by vertically folding a cream cardstock base. Tear strips of patterned papers; adhere to front of card with border sticker to create frame. Randomly stamp vintage-image stamps in black and cranberry inks. Crumple torn piece of red handmade paper; flatten and glue to front of card. Add stamped and torn pieces of patterned paper. Create tag from cream cardstock. Stamp numbers for age; emboss with gold embossing powder and color with colored pencils. Stipple-brush tag with inks; punch hole. Apply reinforcement ring; color ring and card edge with gold paint pen. Glue jewel onto tag, tie organza ribbon through tag into bow; mount tag with foam spacers. Cut out dictionary definition with decorative scissors; color edges with gold paint pen and adhere. Finish with vintage button sticker and gold photo corners.

Trisha McCarty-Luedke, Memory Makers magazine

Supplies: Patterned paper (Design Originals); lace and button stickers (EK Success); illuminated number stamps (All Night Media); ornamental writing stamp (Hero Arts); music stamp (Toybox Rubber Stamps); red jewel (Westrim); handmade paper; gold paint pen (Pilot); decorative scissors (Fiskars); black and cranberry stamping inks; organza ribbon; gold photo corners; gold embossing powder; colored pencils; reinforcement ring; foam spacers; cream cardstock

Happy Birthday

Create this crisp, understated birthday salutation with little more than stamps and patterned paper. Begin with a vertically folded green cardstock base. Cut two blocks from patterned paper; mount to top and bottom of card. Stamp text square and solid square using rust-colored ink on pale green cardstock; stamp solid square with sentiment stamp. Cut out images and mat on rust-colored cardstock; mount. To complete, accent card with green button tied with fiber.

Amy Kennedy for My Sentiments Exactly, Colorado Springs, Colorado

Supplies: Stamps (My Sentiments Exactly); rust ink; button; fibers; cream-colored paper; green, pale and rust cardstocks

...To A Timeless Wonder

Age is but a state of mind, as this artistic card states. Begin with a horizontally folded, textured brown cardstock card base. Ink edges of patterned paper with brown ink and mount to card front. Tear piece of handmade paper and adhere to top of card. Embellish with clock hands secured by brad. Age metal-rimmed tag with walnut ink; coat with clear lacquer and sprinkle with watch parts. Once dry, set eyelet and thread with wire adorned with beads. Adhere along with watch face accent to card front. Print sentiment on ivory cardstock; cut and ink edges with brown stamping ink to complete.

Barbara Vargas, Woodbridge Township, New Jersey

Supplies: Patterned paper (7 Gypsies); textured brown cardstock (Bazzill); watch parts (Jest Charming); metal-rimmed tag; walnut ink; beige handmade paper; wire; beads; clear lacquer; brown stamping ink; brad

Happy Birthday to a
Timeless Wonder

Supplies: Patterned paper (7 Gypsies); rawhide paper (Provo Craft); black ribbon; handmade wire charm; brad; brown stamping ink; cream cardstock

Happy Birthday...

This elegant card harmoniously blends texture and classic simplicity. Begin with a horizontally folded cream cardstock base. Mount patterned and rawhide papers to card front; adhere ribbon where edges meet. Affix handmade wire charm to ribbon with silver brad. Print sentiment on cream cardstock; cut, round corners and ink edges with brown ink. Mount greeting to card front to complete.

Deborah March, Lunenburg County, Nova Scotia, Canada

Surprise Birthday

Poke a little healthy fun at a loved one by incorporating a childhood photo into a "tongue-in-cheek" surprise birthday invitation. Print invitation on cream cardstock. Scan and print childhood photo onto cream cardstock; tear to size and adhere to front of invitation to complete.

Carrie O'Donnell, Newburyport, Massachusetts

Supplies: Cream cardstock; scanned photo

Living proof that things really do get better with age!

Please join us for a SURPRISE 40th 1/2 birthday celebration for

Karen Bedard

Saturday, August 9th
6:30 PM sharp
Upstairs at Sylvan Street Grille
Salisbury, MA

Regrets only to Johnny
at (978) 479-4833 by 8/1/03

Bring your favorite funny Karen story!
We know you all have them!

You're Invited to a Birthday Brunch!

Birthday Brunch
Menu

Beverages:
Orange Juice, Apple Juice, Milk

Fruit:
Oranges, Grapes, Apples, Grapefruit

Breads:
Croissants, Toast, Bagels, Muffins

Main Course:
Eggs Florentine

Supplies: Flower punch (Family Treasures); leaf punch (EK Success); hole punch; embroidery floss; vellum; green, white and yellow cardstocks

Birthday Brunch

Create a lovely invitation with matching menu for a special birthday brunch. The card base is a small horizontally folded piece of green cardstock. Tear bottom edge from card front. Punch flowers from white cardstock and leaves from green cardstock. Punch yellow cardstock flower centers with hole punch. Arrange flowers and leaves and adhere to yellow cardstock rectangle; mat with white cardstock and mount on card front. Print title, party details and menu on vellum. Cut each to size. Place title on card front and secure by hand stitching at corners with floss. Adhere party details to yellow cardstock; accent with punched flower and mount on card's interior. For menu, arrange and adhere flowers and leaves on yellow cardstock rectangle. Triple mat with torn green cardstock, white cardstock and yellow cardstock. Affix printed vellum menu by stitching in corners with floss.

Jennifer Gallacher, Savannah, Georgia

60th Surprise

Beautiful floral patterned paper and lace stickers combine to create an elegant invitation befitting of any birthday milestone. Start with a long rectangle of burgundy cardstock. Fold left edge over to create 1" flap. Cover card front with patterned paper. Print invitation details on buff vellum; cut to size and adhere over patterned paper. Fold flap over and secure with lace sticker. Crochet embroidery floss chain; adhere down front of flap. Thread buttons and adhere along flap front to complete.

Cheryl Uribe, Grapevine, Texas

Supplies: Patterned paper (Anna Griffin); lace sticker (Mrs. Grossman's); embroidery floss; buttons; buff vellum; burgundy cardstock

Celebrate...

This heirloom-quality digital invitation need only be created once for all on your list to enjoy. Here photo-editing software and a scrapbooking CD were utilized to create the card base. First open the image editor of the photo-editing program. Next, choose a background paper or template from a scrapbooking CD, changing color to suit theme. Import decorative elements from a digital scrapbooking CD, changing colors as needed. Finish by adding title, sentiments and journaling with various fonts, using shadows and beveling to create desired effects.

Michelle Shefveland, Sauk Rapids, Minnesota

Supplies: Adobe Photoshop Elements 2.0; background paper, aged envelope, date tag, typewriter keys alphabet set and eyelets (Simply Vintage CD, (www.cottagearts.com); darkroom photo edge treatment (AutoFX Photo/Graphic Edges CD)

Special
{occasions}

chapter 3

Graduate

Here is a dignified graduation card that showcases the many facets of learning with education-oriented patterned papers. Begin with a vertically folded square black cardstock base. Tear bottom edge off front of card. Adhere cut section of patterned paper to interior of card so that it shows along torn front edge. Cut or punch various patterned papers into 2" squares; lightly sand and adhere to front of card in mosaic pattern. Apply adhesive metal letters vertically along right side of card to complete.

Emily Curry Hitchingham, Memory Makers Books

Supplies: Metal letters (K & Company); patterned papers (7 Gypsies); square punch (Emagination Crafts); black cardstock

Congratulations

Golden words of encouragement grace this graduation card. Start with a horizontally folded black cardstock base. Punch corners of patterned paper with corner punch; mount on card. Adhere black slide mount; accent with acrylic word stickers and mortarboard sticker. Stamp polymer clay with sentiment. Trim to size and bake as directed. When cooled, rub with pigment powder and spray with fixative to set. Attach fiber along bottom of card and apply clay accent with foam adhesive.

Janetta Abucejo Wieneke, Memory Makers Books

Supplies: Polymer clay (Polyform Products); stamp (Hero Arts); pigment powders (Ranger); acrylic words (K & Company); mortarboard sticker (Westrim); slide mount (Scrapworks); corner punch (Emagination Crafts); patterned paper (Paper Adventures); fiber; stamping ink; black cardstock; foam spacers.

Graduation

Create a classy and colorful graduation card with stamped organza ribbon. Start with a vertically folded white cardstock card base. Fold front of card over itself so that edge touches card's crease. Adhere red cardstock strip on folded-back portion to create flap. Stamp image onto white cardstock rectangle; add color with a blender pen and markers and double mat with dark blue and white cardstocks. Glue to red flap so that it overlaps card interior. Stamp organza ribbon with mortarboard stamp and let dry; tie into bow and mount above stamped image. Finish by stamping diploma images along bottom edge of card's interior.

Lanae Byers, Mercersburg, Pennsylvania

Supplies: Stamps (source unknown); black and blue stamping inks; blender pen; markers; organza ribbon; white, blue and red cardstocks

Mortarboard

Hats off to the graduate who receives this mortarboard card. Begin with two identical square pieces of patterned paper; adhere together, patterned sides out. Fold glued square in quarters; crease. Open and fold diagonally so that square collapses into itself along creases to form square one-quarter the size of the whole. Adhere black cardstock squares to top and bottom of folded form. Adorn with button and tassel to complete mortarboard. Stamp sentiment inside card.

Jodi Amidei, Memory Makers Books
Inspired by Karissa Thomas, Yakima, Washington

Supplies: Patterned paper (American Traditional Designs, Family Treasures); word stamp (My Sentiments Exactly); tassel (Provo Craft); button, black cardstock

Congratulations

Create a distinguished card for the grad who stands out in the crowd. Begin by cutting black cardstock into a one-sided card base. Stamp three mortarboard images onto a white cardstock square; punch or cut out a fourth image and color with red marker. Mat both stamped cardstock squares on red cardstock; adhere smaller stamped square to larger stamped square with foam adhesive. Stamp title and emboss with white embossing powder.

Kneka Smith, Phoenix, Arizona

Supplies: Mortarboard and word stamp (Stampin' Up!); red marker; black stamping ink; watermark stamping ink; embossing powder; black, white and red cardstocks; foam spacers

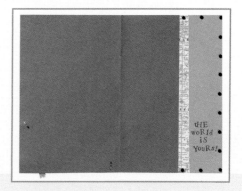

Grad

Send off your graduate in style on his or her new adventure with a little cash tucked inside an interior pocket. Start out with a horizontally folded card base of green cardstock. Adhere map-print paper to front of card. Add four green cardstock rectangles; cover with slide mounts. Place letter stickers in openings and along vellum strip for sentiment; affix vellum strip to card with brads and accent with mortarboard sticker. For interior pocket, cut a strip of green cardstock; line open edge of pocket with strip of map-patterned paper. Stamp message on pocket and attach to card along three sides with brads. Place money in pocket to complete.

Cori Dahmen, Portland, Oregon

Supplies: License plate letter stickers (Sticker Studio); small letter stickers (Colorbök); mortarboard sticker (Westrim); slide mounts (DMD); patterned paper (K & Company); letter stamps (PSX Design); stamping ink; brads; green cardstock; vellum

Graduate

Asian accents create a sense of sophistication, reverence and timelessness in this graduation card. Start with a vertical bifolded piece of red cardstock. Fold right edge over front, creating a 2" section. Print sentiment on patterned paper and cover card front. Layer red ribbon with gold ribbon; adhere across flap. Cover with wide brocade ribbon adhered lengthwise down flap front. Affix tassel to top with brad. Cover interior of card and flap with patterned paper. Stamp patterns along inside edge of flap. Stamp Asian images onto white cardstock and tear to size. Treat inside of card and edges of stamped images with red ink. Stamp rectangles onto black cardstock and emboss with gold extra thick embossing powder. Adhere stamped images on gold embossed rectangles; tear to size and adhere. Tie ribbons around card to complete.

Kathy Fesmire, Athens, Tennessee

Supplies: Patterned paper (Me & My Big Ideas); brocade ribbon and tassel (Wrights); red and gold ribbons (Offray); Asian stamps (Stamp Craft); extra thick embossing powder (Suze Weinberg); rectangle shadow stamp (Stampin' Up!); black and red embossing inks; brad; red cardstock

Please join us for
A Bridal Shower in honor of
Olivia Roberts
On Saturday, May 1
At 2:30 p.m.
Lakeside Country Club
145 Lakeview Ct.
St. Cloud, Minnesota

Jessica Anderson and Amy Roberts

Wedding Invitation

Bring the beauty of embossed paper and vellum into the computer age with this digital card. Begin by opening the image editor of a photo-editing program. Transport background papers, metal heart frames, photo corners and vellum mat into program from digital scrapbooking CD to create background. Alter colors and arrange to suit design. Finish by adding journaling details and embossed words using various fonts and font effects.

Michelle Shefveland, Sauk Rapids, Minnesota

Supplies: Adobe Photoshop Elements 2.0; wedding layout template (Simply Elegant CD, www.cottagearts.com)

Bridal Shower

This easy-to-assemble card looks like you spent a lot of time making it! Start with a rectangle of white cardstock. Layer with patterned paper. Print invitation on a transparency; cut to size. Dry brush pink acrylic paint on back of transparency. Adhere transparency to card front with glue dot. Adhere tulle bow to conceal glue dot to finish.

Valerie Barton, Flowood, Mississippi

Supplies: Patterned paper (K & Company); acrylic paint (Plaid); transparency; pink tulle; white cardstock

You are invited to attend a

Bridal Shower

In honor of

Kaitlyn Barton

Sunday, April 25th

2:00 pm

Colonial Heights Baptist Church

Wedding Dress

Opalescent embossing powder adds high drama to this otherwise subtle card. Begin with a vertically folded white cardstock card base. Adhere patterned vellum to card front. Stamp aluminum sheet and emboss with opalescent embossing powder; adhere. Cut frame from handmade paper; coat with embossing ink and emboss with opalescent embossing powder. String beads and hang across top of paper frame. Affix ribbon across bottom of frame. Adhere assemblage to complete.

Brenda Martinez, Lakewood, Colorado

Supplies: Aluminum sheet (Heritage Handcrafts); patterned vellum (EK Success); handmade paper (Nature's Handmade Paper); dress stamp (Stampin' Up!); holographic embossing powder (Ranger); embossing ink; beads; ribbon; thread; white cardstock

Supplies: Lavender papers and brass templates (Lasting Impressions); opalescent embossing powder (Close To My Heart); flower eyelets (Doodlebug Design); ribbon; chalk; embossing ink; foam adhesive; opalescent and white cardstocks

A Wedding Shower

Emboss a "happy couple" onto a shower invitation. Start with a vertically folded lavender patterned cardstock base. Dry emboss two graduated rectangles using frame stencils from coordinating patterned cardstock; mat one atop the other. Mount at askew angle. Using pearlized paper and brass stencil, dry emboss bride and groom and silhouette. Emboss elements with opalescent embossing powder. Chalk hair and cheek details. Print salutation on pearlized paper; dry emboss with frame stencil and cut out. Set flower eyelets on both ends of the salutation. Thread ribbon through eyelets, knot to secure ends and adhere. Affix embellishment to card front with foam adhesive to complete outside of card. Print invitation details on white cardstock and mount inside card.

Diana Graham, Barrington, Illinois

Carrie Ann and Christopher Robert

Clean, crisp invites like this one are timelessly classy and elegant. Create text in a word processing program and add border. Print on white cardstock and mat on raspberry cardstock. Print starfish clip art image; punch out with square punch. Mat with raspberry cardstock and mount on card front. Adhere acrylic pebble over starfish image to complete.

Carrie O'Donnell, Newburyport, Massachusetts

Supplies: Acrylic pebble (Making Memories); clip art; raspberry and white cardstocks

Madeline and Elijah

Here an informal outdoor wedding is announced with whimsical punched flowers. Create card base from long red cardstock rectangle by folding ends toward center until they meet; crease to create flaps. Craft floral motif from various punched leaves and flowers; punch mini circles for flower centers and adhere. Draw "stitched" stems with white colored pencil. Print invitation text onto white cardstock; cut to size and adhere to interior. Accent with matted punched flower to complete.

Leah Blanco Williams, Kansas City, Missouri

Supplies: Asterisk punch (All Night Media); daisy punch (Carl); mini flower and birch leaf punches (Punch Bunch); mini circle punch(McGill); textured red cardstock (Bazzill); white colored pencil; mustard, white, teal, sage, dark green, light pink and hot pink cardstocks

Wedding Invitation

Add an extra touch of elegance to a postcard-style wedding invitation by creating coordinating vellum sleeves. Print invitation text on white cardstock. Cut to size and mount on patterned paper rectangle. Punch hole in top and tie with coordinating ribbon. Make 3-sided envelope out of matching patterned and embossed vellum. Cut notch in top of envelope for ribbon knot. Slide card into envelope to finish.

Shannon Smith Williams, Galena, Illinois

Supplies: Patterned paper and vellum (K & Company); ribbon; white cardstock

Wedding Card

Any bride and her groom will find this card charming. Begin with a horizontally folded textured pink cardstock base; treat edges with dark pink ink. Chalk embossed paper with pink chalk; machine stitch to card front. Apply pink acrylic paint to strip of copper mesh; let dry. Adhere across card front with glue dots. Print wedding image clip art onto white cardstock, cut to size and emboss with several coats of extra thick embossing powder. When cool, crack by bending and adhere. Tie gingham ribbon and charm across top of card to finish.

Shannon Taylor, Bristol, Tennessee

Supplies: Embossed paper (Jennifer Collection); copper mesh (Making Memories); metal heart (source unknown); extra thick embossing powder (Suze Weinberg); textured pink cardstock (Bazzill); pink acrylic paint; pink gingham ribbon; pink stamping ink; clip art (www.designedtoat.com)

Facing The Future

Customize a pre-made embellishment by adding and taking away elements to best suit your style. Print out invitation on white cardstock. Dry emboss invitation using brass stencil. Cover back of card with patterned paper; punch hole and tie with pink cord. Adhere customized pre-made sticker with foam adhesive. Dry emboss floral bouquet; add chalk accents and adhere to sticker embellishment.

Jenny Moore Lowe, Lafayette, Colorado

Supplies: Wedding dress sticker (Meri Meri); brass template (Lasting Impressions); printed vellum (Treehouse Designs); chalk; pink cord; foam adhesive; patterned paper (source unknown); white cardstock

Supplies: Heart chain template (American Traditional Designs); patterned papers (Paper Patch); corner punch (EK Success); rubber stamp (My Sentiments Exactly); beads (Me & My Big Ideas); stamping ink; pink cardstock; chalk

*May your new lives
together abound in love
today, tomorrow & forever*

May Your New Lives...

This paper chain of hearts symbolizes a never-ending union of love. Begin with a horizontally folded pink cardstock base. Punch corners of card with a corner punch. Glue torn pink rectangle to pink patterned paper rectangle. Using craft knife and template, cut interlocking heart design through both layers. Fold back cut-out sections of hearts to create overlapped effect; adhere and mount to front of card. Hand stitch tiny pearl beads in sets of three along rectangle edge. Stamp with sentiment and chalk edges of card; mount to patterned paper rectangle to complete.

Cori Dahmen, Portland, Oregon

To Love, To Cherish

A glimmering sentiment adorns this classic wedding card. The base is vertically folded light green cardstock. Adhere ribbon along right and left edges of card. Mat pink patterned paper with green paper. "Ink" rubber stamp with white glue; stamp onto vellum. Immediately sprinkle with glitter and shake off excess. Let dry. Tear stamped vellum into strip and attach to complete.

Nicole La Cour, Memory Makers magazine

Supplies: Rubber stamp (DeNami Design); sparkle glitter (Magic Scraps); patterned papers (Creative Imaginations); ribbon; light green cardstock; vellum

Wedding Wishes

Treat embossed paper with acrylic paint to emphasize a lacy pattern. Begin with horizontally folded lavender cardstock. Print sentiment onto white cardstock; stipple-brush edges with lavender ink. Dry-brush embossed paper with white acrylic paint. Once dry, cut out window and treat all edges with black ink. Link rings together and secure to purple ribbon with brads; secure ends to back of embossed paper. Mount sentiment behind window and adhere to card front.

Denise Tucker, Versailles, Indiana

Supplies: Embossed paper (Provo Craft); rings (Wilton); ribbon (Making Memories); white and lavender cardstocks; stamping ink; acrylic paint; brads

Your Wedding Day

Add dimension by cutting out a patterned paper element and "popping" it with foam adhesive. Start with a horizontally folded green cardstock base and layer with patterned paper. Using coordinating patterned paper and vellum, silhouette cut the same flower from both with a craft knife. Align cut-out images; glue together in middle, leaving edges unadhered. Tie pink ribbon around top of card and mount die-cut letter sentiment to complete.

Jodi Amidei, Memory Makers Books

Supplies: Patterned paper and vellum (K & Company); die-cut letters (Quic-Kutz); pink ribbon; foam spacers; green cardstock

Celebrate

This sophisticated wedding card sums up what marriage is all about. Horizontally fold a white cardstock card base. Mat patterned paper with textured purple cardstock. Impress rub-on word onto metal-rimmed tag. Poke holes in ends of tag; tie ribbon bows through both ends and accent with decorative nailheads. Adhere additional ribbon across center of card. Mount tag to complete.

Linda Beeson, Ventura, California

Supplies: Patterned paper (Penny Black); decorative nail heads (American Tag); metal-rimmed tag and rub-on word (Making Memories); ribbon; white and purple cardstocks

Congratulations On Your Wedding Day

Simple design elements lend an air of elegance to this wedding card. Start with a horizontally folded card base of cream cardstock. Print salutation on bottom of card. Layer top two-thirds of card front with textured pearlized paper. Thread charm onto green ribbon and adhere across card front, covering edge of textured paper. Adhere silk flowers behind ribbon charm. Punch bottom corners of card with decorative corner punch.

Deborah March, Lunenburg County, Nova Scotia, Canada

Supplies: Textured pearlized paper (Provo Craft); ribbon charm (Making Memories); ribbon (Offray); silk flowers; vellum; cream cardstock

Congratulations

Here tiered lace creates an artful wedding cake accent. Vertically fold a white cardstock base. Mat pink cardstock rectangle with patterned vellum and mount. Print sentiment onto pink cardstock and double mat with patterned vellum and white cardstock; affix. To create cake embellishment, thread rosebud decorative trim through holes in lace intended for ribbon weaving. Cut into three pieces. Glue thin white ribbon along edges of cut eyelet pieces. Assemble in tiers to create cake layers. Accent with ribbon bow to complete.

Lisa Dixon, East Brunswick, New Jersey

Supplies: Patterned vellum (Paper Adventures); eyelet lace; ribbon; rosebud trim; white and pink cardstocks

Celebrate Love

Try vintage decoupage for a unique and whimsical expression of love. Start with a vertically folded white cardstock card base. Adhere torn images from vintage magazines in collage-style fashion. Apply letter stickers to tiny tags along folded edge for portion of sentiment. Finish by applying additional letter stickers diagonally across collage. Layer with decoupage glue; let dry. Embellish with lace trim, key charm and small frame. Adhere nailheads to letter tags. Mat preprinted quote onto pink cardstock; attach brass photo corners. Mount to card with foam spacers. Stipple-brush sepia ink on quote and lace to age.

Cori Dahmen, Portland, Oregon

Supplies: Circle letter stickers (Foofala); letter stickers (Wordsworth); tags (DMD); book corners (7 Gypsies); circle nailheads (ScrapArts); quote (Karen Foster Design); key charm (Jest Charming); frame (Nunn Design); decoupage adhesive (Plaid); white and pink cardstocks

Supplies: Candy
mold (Wilton); pat-
terned paper (Anna
Griffin); embossed
white cardstock (K &
Company); handmade
papers; cream and
white mulberry papers;
ribbon; toilet paper;
stencil brush

Cupid

Create a dimensional Cupid-inspired card with paper casting. Start with a horizontally folded white cardstock card base. Layer with stripe-patterned paper and cream-colored embossed paper rectangle. See instructions to follow for paper cast accent. Glue cast onto handmade paper with gold accents. Mount entire accent onto embossed paper rectangle. Adhere organza ribbon bow to complete.

Mazie Molinaro, Pittsburgh, Pennsylvania

1 Fill mold with piece of mulberry; spritz with water. Using stencil brush, press mulberry paper into impressions of mold.

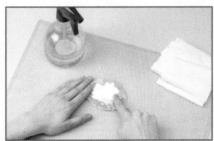

2 Fill in mulberry impression with small bits of water-spritzed toilet paper. Allow to dry thoroughly.

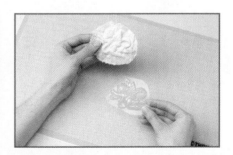

3 Remove impressed image from mold.

Happy Anniversary

Paper flowers lend romantic nostalgia to this anniversary card. Begin with a vertically folded red card-stock card base. Chalk edges with black chalk. Tear one side of a strip of vintage printed paper and adhere along fold of card. Layer with torn strip of floral patterned paper. Roll edges of paper strips. Wrap silk or paper flowers with patterned paper, leaving flower heads exposed; secure with red ribbon. Write sentiment with marker. Using a craft knife, cut slit through front and back of card on right edge; thread white ribbon through and tie to close.

Irene Chadez, Nampa, Idaho

Supplies: Floral patterned paper (Anna Griffin); vintage printed paper; silk or paper flowers; red and white ribbons; black chalk; black marker; red cardstock

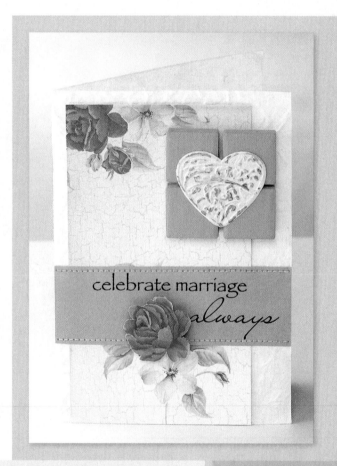

Celebrate Marriage Always

This elegant anniversary card is as timeless as love itself. Its foundation is a vertically folded base of cream-colored handmade paper. Layer front of card with cut section of patterned paper. Paint small square ceramic tiles with green acrylic paint; let dry. Apply antique white acrylic paint to decorative metal heart so that some metal shows through; let dry. Mount tiles to card with tacky tape in mosaic fashion. Adhere metal heart sticker on top of tiles. Print sentiment onto green cardstock; cut into strip and sew to card. Cut out floral element from patterned paper and coat with paper glaze; let dry. Adhere glazed flower to card front with foam spacers.

Diana Hudson, Bakersfield, California

Supplies: Handmade paper (Nature's Handmade Paper); patterned paper (Making Memories); metal heart sticker (Magenta); ceramic tile (Home Depot); green and antique white acrylic paints (Delta); green cardstock; tacky tape; foam spacers

Supplies: *Printed paper (Carolee's Creations); phrase stamps (Biblical Impressions, My Sentiments Exactly); woven labels (Me & My Big Ideas); cranberry and black stamping inks; acrylic words, metal heart charms and letters (K & Company); copper hinges (Foofala); heart sticker (Westrim); musical heart sticker (EK Success); floss; fibers; brads; eyelets; safety pins; heart clip; round clip; vintage magazine; light blue and dark blue cardstocks*

Happy Anniversary Sweetheart

This impressive double accordion-fold card hides secret notes and images of love. See instructions to follow to create and assemble card base. Embellish card with words and images torn from magazines, punched cardstock shapes secured with eyelets, tiny envelopes, heart tags, woven labels, safety pins, hinges, acrylic letters and words, bits of fiber, metal charms and clips. When finished, complete card by randomly stamping phrase stamps. Adhere title printed on transparency and tie closed with braided floss.

Andrea Lyn Vetten-Marley, Aurora, Colorado

1 Cut two 3 x 5" blue paper strips. Score and accordian-fold each strip at 2" intervals.

3 Using a running stitch, stitch two strips together along pierced creases.

2 Align two strips; At second and fourth folds, pierce stitching holes at approximately ¼" intervals.

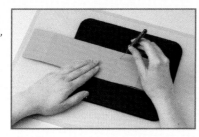

4 Once stitching is complete, stand assemblage upright and collapse into accordian-folded booklet.

To Lift Your Heart

Love is a song in your heart, as this simple yet striking card implies. Begin with a vertically folded black cardstock card base. Layer with cut section of patterned paper. Adhere preprinted transparency sentiments to patterned paper along top and bottom edges. Embellish with pre-made tag to complete.

Amy McGovern, Eldersburg, Maryland

Supplies: Tag (EK Success); transparency words (Magic Scraps); patterned paper (Family Archives); black cardstock

Happy Anniversary

Silk sunflowers and fancy ribbon send warm wishes for an anniversary. Start with a card base of vertically folded cream cardstock. Cover card front with brown cardstock. Cut circle from double-sided yellow cardstock. Mat with larger circle cut from back side of same cardstock. Cut circle in half. Stamp salutation on same yellow cardstock and mat in same fashion as circle. Adhere half of the circle toward top left of card front and remaining half on bottom right so that halves are offset. Tie ribbon lengthwise around front of card. Adhere silk flowers and salutation to ribbon to complete.

Jodi Amidei, Memory Makers Books

Supplies: Double-sided cardstock (Paper Adventures); ribbon (Offray); word stamp (All Night Media); silk flowers; brown stamping ink; cream and brown cardstocks

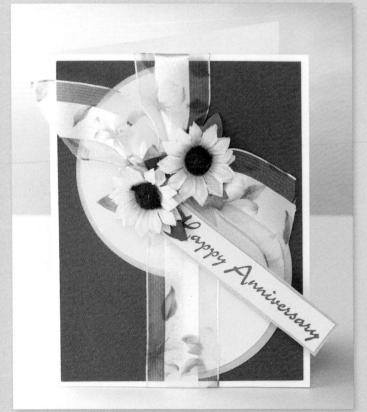

Supplies: Flower and sentiment stamps (Stampin' Up!); watermark ink (Tsukineko); black stamping ink; silver embossing powder; chalk; eyelets; vellum; purple and orange cardstocks

Happy Anniversary

Create a vibrant, contemporary card that celebrates a special anniversary. Start with a vertically folded piece of purple cardstock. Adhere orange cardstock to card front; layer with strip of purple cardstock. Print sentiment on vellum and immediately sprinkle with silver embossing powder; heat emboss. On back side of vellum, stamp flower images onto vellum with watermark ink. Apply chalk to stamped flowers to color. Turn vellum over and attach with eyelets.

Samantha Walker, Battle Ground, Washington

Remember This

Bring back memories of that special day with a card that showcases your wedding photo. Start with a vertically folded card base of tan cardstock. Treat edges of card front with black ink. Crumple metallic paper, flatten and adhere. Highlight embossed paper with gold ink; mount on black paper. Double mat photo on tan and black cardstocks. Apply rub-on sentiment to photo; mount on embossed paper assembly with foam spacers. Coat heart charm with embossing ink and heat emboss with gold embossing powder. Tie ribbon through heart charm and secure on back of embossed paper. Hang key charm from ribbon using invisible thread. Adhere decorative corner charm to upper left corner of embossed paper; adhere entire assembly to card front.

Denise Tucker, Versailles, Indiana Photo: Robert Huddle Photography

Supplies: Metallic paper (Emagination Crafts); embossed paper (Provo Craft); corner charm (Eggery Place); heart charm and letter rub-ons (Making Memories); key charm (7 Gypsies); gold embossing inks; gold embossing powder; black and tan cardstocks

Working Girl

Put an emoticon smile on your favorite working girl's face with this fun card. Start with a horizontally folded green cardstock base. Cover card front with patterned paper. Create title in a word processing program; choose font and size and print onto regular paper. Adhere printed title to green cardstock using temporary adhesive. Cut out letters and remove printed portion; adhere to card base. Chalk letters and edges of card front to complete.

Leah Blanco Williams, Kansas City, Missouri

Supplies: Patterned paper (Chatterbox); chalk; green cardstock

They Found The Treasure In You

The detail throughout this card is a treasure hunt in itself! Start with an 8 x 8" square of torn burgundy handmade paper; tear corners to create octagonal shape. Cut natural handmade paper in a smaller shape; mount over burgundy paper. Fold two opposite corners toward middle until overlapping, leaving a 3" unfolded interior section. Layer with a torn strip of dark green handmade paper. Fold right flap over; pierce holes along flap edge through all layers and stitch to card's interior with hemp. Stitch second flap, accenting every other stitch with a bead. Do not sew to card's interior. Affix metal label holder to right flap with eyelets; glue metal letters at top and bottom of interior and vertically along left flap to form sentiment. Tie fibers adorned with skeleton keys along flap crease. Attach metal handle to left flap; wrap card with fiber strung through handle and label holder eyelet, tying in a bow to secure.

Andrea Lyn Vetten-Marley, Aurora, Colorado

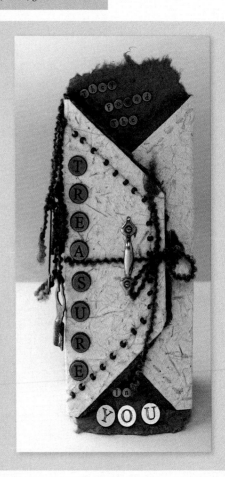

Supplies: Burgundy, dark green and natural handmade papers (Nature's Handmade Paper); metal handle (Foofala); label holder (Nunn Design); alphabet charms (Making Memories); metal letters (K & Company); keys (EK Success, Westrim); fibers; beads; hemp; eyelets

Good Luck On Your New Job

File this card under "cute." Start off with a vertically folded card base of maroon cardstock. Mount strip of black cardstock down center. Adhere mini manila file folders onto card front. Create sentiment using variety of embellishment letters, adhering on file fronts to create sentiment. Insert handwritten notebook paper sections into two file folders. Finish by securing paper clips to black strip.

Jill Tennyson, Lafayette, Colorado

Supplies: Metal letters (Making Memories); typewriter letters (Creative Imaginations); acrylic letters (K & Company); mini file folders (DMD); round and regular paper clips; handwritten notes on paper; black and maroon cardstocks

Congrats

Cast out this fun pop-out card to someone who has just caught a great new job. Start with a vertically folded ivory cardstock base. Trim 1" from edge of front flap. See directions that follow to re-create pop-out feature. Tear strips of dark green and ginger cardstocks and mount to card front, folding around right edge and continuing on interior of card. Using various stamps, stamp texture onto rust and dark green cardstocks, blue-green patterned paper and copper paper. Free-hand cut fish tail, fins and scales from stamped papers. Adhere to front of card with foam spacers. On interior, compete freehand design of paper-pieced fish. Cut oval shape from stamped cardstock. With card completely open and flat, glue stamped oval over slit in card. Turn card over; with craft knife, remake slit through cardstock oval using existing slit as guide. Open card and refold fish's mouth in same direction as underlying folds. Adhere strip of copper paper along right edge of card. Create title and sentiment with letter stickers. Finish card by handcrafting fishing line using fly made from twisted wire and fiber and floss line that is adhered to back of card.

Torrey Miller, Thornton, Colorado

Supplies: Patterned paper (Karen Foster Design); copper paper (Paper Garden); textured mat and moldable stamps (Clearsnap); letter stickers (Colorbök); brown stamping ink; fibers; wire; foam spacers; ginger, dark green, rust and ivory cardstocks

1 Using a ruler, draw a 2" square over crease. Use a craft knife to cut horizontal slit from left to right corners.

2 Fold card back together. Bend back flaps.

3 Open card. Using finger, press folds toward center to create fish's mouth.

We Moved!

This unique card uses actual packing material that the artist had around the house during her recent move. Start off with a cardboard rectangle. Strip the front layer off to reveal the ribs underneath. Add text to photo using Microsoft Picture It software. Print out photo on regular paper and tear into rough rectangle shape. Attach photo to card front with staples. Add strips of duct tape in opposite corners to complete.

Sam Cousins, Trumbull, Connecticut

Supplies: Cardboard; staples; duct tape; printer paper

We've Moved

Give your new address to special friends with this elegant card. Begin with a vertically folded cream cardstock base. Create splattered background with a brush-tip pen and a sprayer bulb, or by applying brown acrylic paint to a toothbrush and dragging your thumb across it to disperse flecks. Add black cardstock border along left side of card. Stamp grid pattern with shadow stamp and beige chalk ink; allow to dry. Using a blender pen, transfer photocopied clip art image of house onto card. Print title onto black cardstock using opaque printer ink; cut into long oval shape and adhere. Secure key embellishment with rubber band or wire. Glue keyhole onto bottom of card to finish.

MaryJo Regier, Memory Makers Books

Supplies: Charms (Li'l Davis Designs); shadow stamp (Hero Arts); sprayer bulb (source unknown); beige chalk ink; brown brush pen; house clip art; blender pen; cream and black cardstocks; rubber band

Best Wishes

If only painting a house were really this much fun! Kitschy images from a vintage magazine bring this card to life. The base card is made from vertically-folded brown cardstock. Add a torn strip of light brown patterned paper along right edge. Tear images from magazine and mount onto torn black cardstock. Completely cover image and torn mat with watermark or embossing ink. Heat emboss with several layers of extra thick embossing powder, applying one layer at a time. When cooled, crack embossed image by bending with hands. Ink torn mat edges with gold ink. Adhere embossed pictures to card base; set eyelets in zigzag pattern down right side of card. Add eyelets to top and bottom of left side of card. Thread fiber through eyelets on both right and left sides. Secure transparency title onto light brown patterned paper with eyelets. Handwrite remainder of title on patterned paper. Ink edges of title with brown ink. Attach remainder of title to bottom of card with eyelets.

Andrea Lyn Vetten-Marley, Aurora, Colorado

Supplies: Patterned paper (Me & My Big Ideas); fiber (Timeless Touches); clear extra thick embossing powder (Suze Weinberg);watermark ink; gold ink; eyelets; transparency; images from vintage magazine

Welcome To The Real World

Welcome friends into the world of homeowner responsibilities with this fun card. Start with a tall green vertically folded card base. Cover with red handmade paper leaving ¼" border all around. Cut out image from a vintage magazine; adhere it to red background. Clip out random "ransom" letters to form title; glue them to yellow cardstock. Trim excess cardstock from around words. Embellish card with gingham ribbon across bottom. Accent card with a copper nameplate and mini drawer pull.

Kelli Noto, Centennial, Colorado

Supplies: Handmade red paper (Nature's Handmade Paper) copper nameplate (Magic Scraps); copper drawer pull (Foofala); ribbon; green and yellow cardstocks; image and letters from vintage magazine

Shower

Ten little fingers and ten little toes add the perfect touch to this dimensional invitation. Begin with a horizontally folded pink cardstock base. Layer with printed transparency; attach with brads. Tear, crumple and flatten two sections of white cardstock; mount. Apply rub-on letters to unfolded paper tiles; assemble tiles and mount on one torn cardstock strip. Place hands and feet stickers on remaining piece of cardstock. Stamp or print shower information on inside of card to complete.

Holle Wiktorek, Reunion, Colorado

Supplies: Folded tiles, rub-ons, stickers (Creative Imaginations); pink mini brads

A Baby Shower

Incorporate a crocheted flower accent to lend a cheerful touch to a baby shower invitation. Make this one-sided card using a white cardstock rectangle base; print information and mat on pink cardstock. Tie gingham ribbon around matted card; adhere crocheted element to metal-rimmed tag and affix. Mount card on black cardstock.

Betsy Sammarco, New Canaan, Connecticut

Supplies: Crocheted flower (Cut-It-Up); tag (EK Success); gingham ribbon; white, black and pink cardstocks

Baby Shower

Feature shower information inside a charming frame-style card. Layer a vertically folded white cardstock card base with navy blue cardstock. Cut a large window in card front. To create frame border, stamp duck image onto white cardstock. Using a craft knife, silhouette-cut right side of stamped image; use a ruler and craft knife to create half-inch frame to fit window. Attach two eyelets in upper left corner of card; thread ribbon through and tie into bow. Stamp another duck image onto spare white cardstock; cut wing and beak with a craft knife. Color duck and frame; mount wing and beak to duck with foam adhesive. Stamp fill-in shower information on inside of card to complete.

Cori Dahmen, Portland, Oregon

Supplies: Duck stamp (EK Success); invitation stamp (My Sentiments Exactly); stamping ink; eyelets; colored pencils; ribbon; white and navy cardstocks

A Baby Shower

This endearing digital card incorporates safety pins, buttons and metal-rimmed tags as cute as the real thing. Begin by opening the image editor of a photo-editing program. Import baby page elements from digital scrapbooking CD template. Alter colors and arrange elements as desired. Add journaling and title to complete.

Michelle Shefveland, Sauk Rapids, Minnesota

Supplies: Jasc Paint Shop Pro 8.1; Baby Moments Downloadable Page Pak (www.cottagearts.com)

"I am a Child of God &
He has sent me here."

I Am A Child Of God...

Make a mold of Baby's foot to create a beautiful 3-D paper casting. Start with a pre-made, torn-edge card. Mount two strips of patterned paper to card front. Print sentiment on vellum; cut to size and adhere. To create paper casting, make a plaster cast of Baby's foot using a plaster casting kit available from hobby and craft stores. Take cast to a pottery store; form clay mold from plaster casting. After mold is fired, it can be used repeatedly. To create casted paper, blend white cardstock and water in blender. Prepare clay mold by spraying with unflavored cooking spray. Place paper pulp into mold and press with sponge to absorb excess water. Continue adding pulp until foot is filled over rim of mold. Heat in microwave for 1-3 minutes. Remove and gently pry casting from mold with knife edge. Allow cast to dry completely before adhering to card.

Aimee Wright, Parkville, Missouri

Supplies: Pre-made card (source unknown); patterned paper (Frances Meyer); vellum; plaster casting kit; clay; water; white cardstock

Taylor Presents...

You'll leave lucky recipients of this sweet birth announcement tickled pink. Start by printing information onto textured pink cardstock; cut into a rectangle and mat with black cardstock. Thread gingham ribbon through two holes at top of card to form a French knot. Print photo onto textured cardstock and trim; add eyelet and hang from ribbon with jump ring. Treat edges of pink background and photo with black ink to complete.

Janet Hopkins, Frisco, Texas

Supplies: Ribbon; black stamping ink; pink and black textured cardstocks (Bazzill); eyelet; jump ring

Taylor S[...]kins
is proud to [...] birth
of [...]

Born June 12 [...]03 @ 7:55 am
8.2 Pounds – 20 inches long

Rachel

Welcome a little girl into the world with this elegant card. Start with a vertically folded white cardstock base. Layer with cut section of corrugated paper on left side and patterned paper on right side. Stipple-brush laser-cut tag with pink ink; treat edges with brown ink and accent with ribbon. Stamp watch image onto tag with brown ink, then date stamp in pink ink; emboss date with clear embossing powder. String alphabet beads on fiber to spell name; attach to tag with mini clothespins. Ink small heart tag using aforementioned techniques; handwrite birth weight. Set flower eyelet and tie off with fiber. Treat small silk flowers with brown ink. Adhere all elements to card including tiny gold frame for title. Complete card by inking edges of entire card with brown ink.

Kelly Angard, Highlands Ranch, Colorado

Supplies: Laser-cut tag (Cardeaux); heart tag (DMD); frame (Nunn Design); patterned paper (PSX Design); watch stamp (Rubber Stampede); November stamp (My Sentiments Exactly); number stamps (Hero Arts); clothespins, alphabet beads and flowers (Westrim); flower eyelet (Doodlebug Design); ribbon; fiber; brown and pink stamping inks; clear embossing powder; corrugated paper; white cardstock

Wanted!

Announce your new baby in the style of a Wild West wanted poster! To make this postcard-style card, start with a brown cardstock base. Print information onto beige cardstock; tear into rough rectangle. Chalk and fold over edges to create parchment effect. Mat photo on brown cardstock. Secure photo to mat with clear photo corners. Finish with 3-D themed sticker.

Stephanie Ray, Little Rock, Arkansas

Supplies: Boot sticker (EK Success); photo corners (Pioneer); chalk; brown and beige cardstocks.

James David Moore

Die cutting makes putting this all-boy card together a breeze. This one-sided announcement begins with a long rectangle of blue patterned paper. Print information on top two-thirds of white cardstock; die cut baby feet at bottom and cut into rectangle. Thread ribbon through two holes at top of cardstock to form French knot. Mat on blue patterned rectangle to complete.

Tammy Moore, Dallas, Texas

Supplies: Patterned paper (Colorbök); feet die cut (Accu-Cut); ribbon (Offray); white cardstock

Congratulations

Images of a baby's arrival adorn this pretty pink card. Begin with an elongated white cardstock rectangle to create a bifold base. Make first horizontal fold at bottom edge of card to create flap. Make second horizontal fold by folding top edge of card over to meet bottom flap. Line inside of card with patterned paper. Mount contrasting pink patterned papers to top and bottom flaps; stitch with sewing machine. Set eyelets in center of both flaps where edges meet. Adhere photo stickers to green patterned paper rectangle; mount with foam spacers. Thread ribbon through eyelets and tie flaps closed. Stamp with sentiment to complete.

Mellette Berezoski, Crosby, Texas

Supplies: Patterned papers (Chatterbox); photo stickers (Pebbles); word stamp (Stampin' Up!); stamping ink; eyelets; ribbon; white cardstock; foam spacers

Supplies: Patterned paper (7 Gypsies); expression sticker (Creative Imaginations); So Sweet sticker (EK Success); rubber stamp (Stamp Craft); metal letter tags and safety pins (Making Memories); blue stamping ink; clear embossing powder; eyelets; navy, light blue and cream cardstocks

A Boy's A Blessing

Welcome a little boy with this sweet card. Start with a horizontally folded baby blue cardstock base. Layer with cream-colored cardstock rectangle. Set three eyelets along lower right edge of navy blue rectangle. Attach metal letter tags to eyelets with safety pins. Tear strip of patterned paper and mount on navy blue cardstock rectangle. Stamp footprints onto patterned paper; emboss with clear embossing powder. Apply transparent phrase sticker and adhere embellished rectangle. Finish with additional word stickers.

Aimee Grenier, Hinton, Alberta, Canada

It's A Girl!

Make a card that's all wrapped up in a pretty bow for a new little girl. Start with horizontally folded pink cardstock. Stamp image onto white cardstock rectangle; mat with dark pink cardstock. Wrap with ribbon bow and mount to card front. Punch heart out of patterned tag; mat with white cardstock. Set eyelet in tag; tie to ribbon bow with fiber. Stamp sentiments onto tag and stamped cardstock.

Stephanie David
Astorville, Ontario, Canada

Supplies: Patterned paper (Provo Craft); word stamps (Hero Arts); background stamp (Memories); heart punch (EK Success); tag (Stampin' Up!); pink and black stamping inks; textured light and dark pink cardstocks (Bazzill); eyelet; ribbon; fiber; white cardstock

Boy

Although simply stated, this card says it all! Begin with a pre-made window card, or create a window in a vertically folded white cardstock card base using a craft knife. Trim blue patterned paper around window opening. Adhere letter stickers and button to inside of card to create sentiment, centering "boy" in window.

Susan Cyrus, Broken Arrow, Oklahoma

Supplies: Pre-made card base (Me & My Big Ideas); patterned paper (Chatterbox); letter stickers (Wordsworth); button

Hooray 4 You

Send good tidings times two to the lucky parents of twins. Begin with a horizontally folded white cardstock base. Cover with patterned paper; adhere ribbon to top and bottom of card front, affixing ends under patterned paper. Mount to card. Apply letter stickers and metal numbers to ribbon to form sentiment. Attach heart-shaped clips with brads. "Hang" baby clothes accents from heart clip to finish.

Shanna Lamb, Mesa, Arizona

Supplies: Patterned paper (Rusty Pickle); heart clips and metal numbers (Making Memories); letter stickers (Colorbök); baby clothes accents (EK Success); gingham ribbon; brads; white cardstock

Welcome To Retirement

Nothing embodies retirement quite like a pink plastic flamingo. Echo this icon on a card that commemorates such a milestone. Begin with a dark green horizontally folded card base. Add a strip of gingham-patterned paper across the middle and a triangular piece of green striped paper along the top. Adhere lime green rickrack along edge of green patterned paper. See instructions below to create polymer clay accents. Mat by adhering accents to torn cardstock; mat again with white cardstock trimmed with decorative scissors. Complete sentiment with letter stickers.

Torrey Miller, Thornton, Colorado

Supplies: *Polymer clay (Polyform Products); patterned paper, letter stickers (Colorbök); rickrack (Me & My Big Ideas); stamps (Museum of Modern Rubber); black and red dye-based inks; green, white and red cardstocks*

1 Roll out polymer clay to ⅛" inch thickness. Using solvent based ink, stamp image onto clay; cut into rectangle.

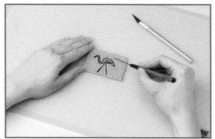

2 Using piercing tool, etch concentric lines around stamped image. Bake clay according to manufacturer instructions and allow to cool.

3 Using cotton swab, rub edges of stamped clay piece with red chalk. Mount finished piece on torn red cardstock with double-sided tape.

Supplies: Paige Mini letters (QuicKutz); celebrate word, twill and metal spiral (7 Gypsies); square nail heads (Chatterbox); wooden sun (Hobby Lobby); clip art (Dover Publications); transparency; ribbon; cardstock; blender pen; glue dots

...Where Every Day Is Saturday

You can almost feel the relaxing warmth of retirement with this sunny, funny card. Its base is horizontally folded yellow cardstock. Add a black strip of cardstock across the bottom about ¼" from the edge. Use a blender pen to transfer photocopied clip art image onto cardstock background. Create calendar in a word processing program; print along with remainder of title onto transparency. Cut out calendar and title and adhere to background with glue dots and decorate with square nailheads. Finish title by gluing die-cut letters along top of black cardstock strip. Adorn with ribbon, metal spiral accent and preprinted twill tape. Glue painted wooden sun accent on top of card to complete.

Torrey Miller, Thornton, Colorado

Congratulations On Your Retirement

Congratulate that special retiree with this elegant card. Start off with a vertically folded speckled beige cardstock base. Ink all outside and interior edges with black ink. Print sentiments onto transparency. Adhere fabric strip down left side of card front. Cut printed transparency into strip and adhere down right side of card front. Cover crease with cream ribbon. Ink speckled beige cardstock strip; cut and adhere across top of card front. Cut sentiment printed on transparency and place under label holder; secure to strip with decorative snaps. For card's interior, mount additional piece of fabric paper to right side. Cut inked cardstock strip and printed transparency and attach with decorative snaps.

Lisa Dixon, East Brunswick, New Jersey

Supplies: Label holder and decorative snaps (Making Memories); speckled beige cardstock (Club Scrap); fabric paper (K & Company); cream ribbon; transparency; stamping ink

Supplies: Patterned paper (Sweetwater); letter stamps (Ma Vinci's); ball chain; fiber; wire; stamping ink; textured light blue cardstock (Bazzill); tan, white and brown cardstocks

Retiring?

Encourage a new retiree to kick up his or her feet and relax. Begin with a horizontally-folded brown cardstock base. Cover card front with patterned paper and torn textured cardstock strips to mimic beach scene. Stamp title onto white cardstock rectangle and mat with torn tan cardstock. Create "hammock" by tying fibers together in knots at their junctions. Attach to card with tiny ball chain secured with wire U pins.

Jill Tennyson, Lafayette, Colorado

Thinking
{of you}

chapter 4

Hello Friend

When you can't catch up over tea in person, send the next-best thing. Start off with a vertically folded base of black cardstock. Cut rough rectangle of red patterned paper; zigzag stitch to card front with sewing machine. Cut letters from patterned paper and adhere to top of card; set tiny eyelets to embellish. For tea cup, begin with a long strip of brown patterned paper; fold ends toward each other to middle. Turn over and cut scooped section from top to create lip of cup. Adhere to card front and fill with tea bag, stir stick, honey packet and tea wrapper. Punch two circles from paper, adhere together and form arch for cup handle; affix under right edge of cup. Apply die-cut letters on cup bottom to complete.

Cori Dahmen, Portland, Oregon

Supplies: Red patterned paper (Magenta); brown patterned paper (source unknown); letter paper (Li'l Davis Designs); die-cut letters (QuicKutz); tiny eyelets; tea paraphernalia; black thread; black cardstock

Supplies: Coffee stamps (Club Scrap); plastic letters (Westrim); brown and rust stamping inks; library pocket (Anima Designs); eyelet; ribbon; pumpkin and cinnamon-colored cardstocks

Hello

This card is perfect for that coffee-lover in your life. Start with a cinnamon-colored cardstock rectangle. Stamp coffee-themed images onto library pocket and adhere to card. Apply plastic letter tiles to library pocket for sentiment. Cut rectangle from pumpkin-colored cardstock to fit inside pocket; add eyelet to corner, tie with ribbon, write message and slip into pocket to complete.

Colleen Adams, Huntington Beach, California

Hello

This "hello" is heralded with understated style. Begin with a horizontally folded textured butterscotch cardstock. Cut patterned paper rectangle; adhere to card front. Cut squares from green and yellow cardstocks; overlap, detail with black marker and adhere. Cut four circles from patterned paper and adhere to squares. Create salutation with letter stickers on yellow sqaure.

Kristy Lee, Alpine, Utah

Supplies: Patterned paper (MOD); letter stickers (SEI); textured butterscotch-colored cardstock (Bazzill); black marker; yellow and green cardstocks

Just A Quick Note…

Put a song in someone's heart with this card. Start with a vertically folded patterned paper base. Stamp and emboss musical score on vellum; cut and adhere to card front. Print title on pale green cardstock; spray with sparkle spray and mat on olive green cardstock. Diagonally fold long vellum strip over and over. Adhere to dark olive cardstock strip and mount. Dot dimensional metallic paint along vellum and on title. Stamp musical note on pale green paper; paint with dimensional metallic paint, silhouette and adhere with foam adhesive.

Oksanna Pope, Los Gatos, California

Supplies: Patterned paper (Design Originals); music note and score stamps (All Night Media); sparkle spray and dimensional metallic paint (Duncan); embossing ink; gold embossing powder; vellum; pale green and dark green cardstocks

Hello

Here's a hello card that makes a fashion statement! Begin with a horizontally folded card base of black cardstock. Adhere strips of coordinating patterned papers; detail with glitter glue and let dry. Collage microscope slide with patterned papers, trimming excess. Layer with second microscope slide; secure all sides with black electrical tape, apply glitter glue and let dry. Tie torn strip of pink fabric around card; thread piece of black tulle through knot. Affix microscope slide to card front with foam adhesive. Print salutation on transparency; paint back side with pink acrylic paint, let dry, cut and adhere.

Jodi Amidei, Memory Makers Books

Supplies: Patterned papers (Two Busy Moms); glitter glue (Ranger); microscope slides; pink acrylic paint; pink fabric; black tulle; electrical tape; transparency; black cardstock

Hello

This fun and funky card says "hello" with style. Create the card base from vertically folded textured lavender cardstock. Adhere strip of patterned paper down right edge of card front; cover remainder of card front with contrasting patterned paper. Apply a variety of letter stickers to top of card to create greeting. Distress pre-made metal flowers with sandpaper; accent with buttons and adhere to bottom of card to complete.

Melissa Lambino, West Lafayette, Indiana

Supplies: Striped patterned paper, letter stickers, buttons (Doodlebug Design); green patterned paper (Kangaroo & Joey); metal flower charms (Making Memories); textured lavender cardstock (Bazzill); sandpaper

Hi

Cool colors and clean lines combine to make this happy hello card. Begin with a long white cardstock rectangle. Fold ends toward each other to meet off-center in card front; crease flaps. Cover flaps with contrasting patterned papers. Adhere word block to right edge of left flap, partially overlapping right flap. Affix acrylic flowers to card front with colored brads. Print sentiment on light blue cardstock; trim to size; adhere on inside of card to complete.

Mellette Berezoski, Crosby, Texas

Supplies: Patterned papers, word block, acrylic flowers (KI Memories); colored brads (Making Memories); white and light blue cardstocks

I Miss Your Face

This striking card is composed of elegant images and a sophisticated stamp design. Begin with a vertically folded black cardstock card base. Tear patterned paper into rectangle; color edges with gold leafing pen and adhere to card front. Stamp three face images onto cream-colored cardstock. Add color to two images with marker. Cut images, mat with black cardstock and arrange, mounting two images with foam adhesive. Print sentiment onto vellum; tear into strip and affix with tiny eyelets. Cover dominoes with floral patterned paper; color edges with gold leafing pen. Using lettering template, color letters onto dominoes with marker for portion of sentiment; adhere.

Cori Dahmen, Portland, Oregon

Supplies: Script patterned paper (K & Company); floral patterned paper (Me & My Big Ideas); face stamps (Hampton Art Stamps); dominoes (Sunday International); lettering template (Wordsworth); gold leafing pen (Krylon); tiny eyelets; vellum; markers; black stamping ink; foam adhesive; white and black cardstocks

Time Stands Still

Show how slowly the minutes pass while you are apart with this clever card. Begin with a vertically folded tan cardstock base. Cover card front with red and diamond patterned papers. Adhere tied ribbon where patterned papers meet. Cut letters from patterned paper and hand stitch to top of card. Embellish pre-made clock face with letter stickers and clock hands affixed with brad; adhere clock to card front. Attach punch label with brads to complete.

Diana Hudson, Bakersfield, California

Supplies: Diamond patterned paper (Me & My Big Ideas); red patterned paper (Carolee's Creations); letter paper (Li'l Davis Designs); acrylic letter stickers (K & Company); clock hands and face (Limited Edition); punch label (Dymo); ribbon; black thread, mini brads; tan cardstock

Miss You Loads

Construct this tag and pocket card using a template and metallic copper cardstock. Collage tag and pocket with cut-out elements from vintage and floral patterned papers; rub each with copper pigment powder. Color edges of plastic letter tiles with copper leafing pen. Adhere plastic letter tiles and letter stickers to tag for sentiment. Tie fibers through hole in top of tag. Fold pocket according to template and secure pocket flap with decorative brad. Slip tag into pocket to complete.

Jodi Amidei, Memory Makers Books

Supplies: *Metallic copper cardstock (Paper Adventures); vintage patterned paper (7 Gypsies); floral paper (PSX Design); card template (Wordsworth); plastic letter tiles (Westrim); letter stickers (K & Company); fibers (Timeless Touches); copper leafing pen (Krylon); copper pigment powder (Jacquard); square copper brad*

Miss You

Show someone special that you miss him or her no matter the time of the year. Begin with a horizontally folded cinnamon cardstock base. Layer with beige cardstock and patterned paper strip. Stamp identical image on blue and green cardstocks; cut blue cardstock into rectangle and crop green cardstock. Align images, mounting cropped image with foam adhesive. Apply rub-on letters for sentiment. Ink edges of blue cardstock with brown ink and detail with clear lacquer. Affix photo turns with brads to secure assemblage. Randomly affix acrylic month and year stickers to complete.

Torrey Miller, Thornton, Colorado

Supplies: *Patterned paper (Chatterbox); stamp (Stampabilities); month/year stickers and rub-on letters (Creative Imaginations); photo turns (7 Gypsies); clear lacquer; mini brads; brown stamping ink; foam spacers; beige, blue, green and cinnamon cardstocks*

Miss You

Understated beauty adorns this heartfelt card. Start with a tall vertically folded card base of textured white cardstock. Treat edges with gray ink. Print salutation on green cardstock; cut and mount on card front and embellish with vase sticker. Adhere real twigs in vase to complete.

Emily Garza, Layton, Utah

Supplies: *Vase sticker (Card Connection); gray stamping ink; twigs; textured white cardstock (Bazzill); green cardstock*

Friends

Vintage-style papers and a mosaic arrangement lend visual interest to this card. Begin with vertically folded black ribbed cardstock for base. Square-punch or cut a variety of vintage-themed patterned papers; treat edges with gray and brown inks. Ink edges of textured beige cardstock with brown ink; arrange and adhere squares. Distress assemblage with brown ink; accent with tied ribbon and mount. Paint pre-made metal word with black acrylic paint. Let dry and sand gently with sandpaper. Affix word to card front with black staples to complete.

Janet Hopkins, Frisco, Texas

Supplies: Patterned papers (Anna Griffin, Li'l Davis Designs, 7 Gypsies); black ribbed and textured beige cardstocks (Bazzill); metal word, black staples (Making Memories); gray and brown stamping inks; black acrylic paint; ribbon

Supplies: All rubber stamps (PSX Design); bamboo clip (Magic Scraps); heart charm (Halcraft); speckled rust cardstock (Club Scrap); copper, black and brown stamping inks; antiquities embossing powder (Ranger); clear embossing powder; copper eyelets; copper wire; fibers; black, ginger and pumpkin cardstocks

...To Grow Old Friends

Honor a seasoned friendship with this striking card. Begin with a card base of vertically folded beige cardstock. Stamp speckled rust cardstock with a word block and mount on card front. Cut square from black cardstock; tear in half diagonally to create triangle pocket and affix with copper eyelets. Stamp and emboss sentiment onto ginger-colored cardstock; tear out, adhere to pocket and accent with bamboo clip. Cut tag shape from pumpkin-colored cardstock; stamp and emboss with tree image. Stipple-brush brown ink onto tag and sentiment edges. Treat edges of card, tag and pocket with copper ink. Tie tag with fibers and hang metal heart charm with copper wire. Slip tag into pocket to finish.

Nancy Walker, Nashville, Tennessee

Flower Of Friendship

A pre-made card and pocket make it easy to assemble this elegant friendship card. Personalize it by stamping sentiment on card. Tear strip of patterned vellum, adhere across top of card and tie with fiber. Stipple-brush brown ink along top edge. Accent with metal dragonfly. Adhere patterned vellum to pocket; slide card into pocket to complete.

Shari Frost-Job, Buffalo, Minnesota

Supplies: Pre-made card and pocket (Foofala); patterned vellum (Autumn Leaves); phrase stamp (www.jodypoesy.com); dragonfly charm (www. maudeandmillie.com); fiber; brown stamping ink

Friends

Celebrate a special relationship with this fun, friendly card. Start with a long, horizontally folded card base of white cardstock. Run metallic green and embossed vellum papers through adhesive application machine. Cut into thin strips and mount vertically on card front. Cut shape from textured pale yellow cardstock. Arrange letters and affix with green conchos. Mat assemblage with green metallic paper and mount to card front with foam adhesive.

Brenda Martinez, Lakewood, Colorado

Supplies: Green metallic paper and embossed vellum (Paper Adventures); acrylic letter (K & Company); letters and colored conchos (Scrapworks); foam spacers; textured yellow cardstock (Bazzill); white cardstock

Friendships...

Nontraditional scrapbooking items and complementary colors add impact to this friendship card. Begin with a tall, vertically folded card base of lavender cardstock. Cover card front with patterned vellum, leaving border on three sides. Handwrite sentiment with marker on vellum; let dry. Disassemble silk flower and use 3-4 petal groups for embellishment; set eyelet in center. Wrap purple leather strip around card; thread through flower's eyelet and knot.

Irene Chadez, Nampa, Idaho

Supplies: Patterned vellum (Chatterbox); silk flower; purple leather strip; eyelet; marker; lavender cardstock

You N Me

Transfer an image to packing tape to create a fun card that says "togetherness." Start with a square horizontally folded purple cardstock base. Layer interior with patterned paper. Cut away half of card front diagonally. Adhere acrylic letters to interior; stipple-brush with lavender ink and along edges of flap. Stamp word onto left side of card front. Construct pea pod from dark green cardstock and peas from light green cardstock; cover with acrylic circles. Assemble, embellish with wire and adhere with foam spacers. For image transfer, adhere clear packing tape over black-and-white, color photocopied or print media image. Burnish with fingernail; soak taped image in warm water for several minutes. When saturated, completely rub paper off back of tape to reveal transfer. Cut to size and adhere to card front.

Torrey Miller, Thornton, Colorado

Supplies: Patterned paper (Pebbles); acrylic letters (Creative Imaginations); acrylic circles (K & Company); word stamp (My Sentiments Exactly); circle punch (Family Treasures); lavender stamping ink; wire; photocopy of photo; packing tape; foam spacers; light green, dark green and purple cardstocks

True Blue

What color is friendship? True blue, of course. Begin with a vertically folded tan cardstock base. Cover card front with patterned paper. Die cut patterned paper circle; detail edge with copper leafing pen. Coat circle with several coats of extra thick embossing powder; let cool, then bend with hands to crack. Mount on sanded blue paper square; attach with brads. Detail edges of card front with copper leafing pen. Tie gingham ribbon around card's crease to finish.

Diana Hudson, Bakersfield, California

Supplies: Patterned paper, die-cut circle, blue paper (Carolee's Creations); copper leafing pen (Krylon); extra think embossing powder (Suze Weinberg); mini brads; gingham ribbon; tan cardstock

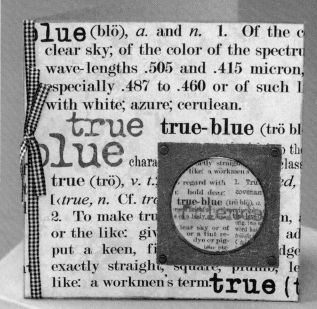

Friends We Are Today...

Here is a card perfect for any girlfriend. Begin with a vertically folded white cardstock card base. Stamp image onto metal-rimmed tag; thread onto organza ribbon. Mat patterned paper with black cardstock. Adhere ribbon and tag across and mount on card front. Stamp sentiment on bottom half of card to complete.

Sharyn Tormanen, Howell, Michigan

Supplies: Patterned paper (7 Gypsies); girls stamp (All Night Media); sentiment stamp (River City Rubber Works); black stamping ink; organza ribbon; white and black cardstocks

Friends we are today
and friends we'll always be
for I am wise to you, and
you can see through me.

Solemates

Step out with this fun friendship card. Start with a horizontally folded card base of white cardstock. Cover card front with patterned paper. Stamp image onto white cardstock rectangle; mat with red cardstock and mount. Adhere gingham bow to shoe image to complete.

Diana Hudson, Bakersfield, California

Supplies: Patterned paper (KI Memories); stamp (My Sentiments Exactly); red stamping ink; gingham ribbon; red and white cardstocks

SHOES
SOLEMATES
STEPPING OUT
HEAD OVER HEELS
YOU'RE A SHOE I'
SENSE IN YOUR SHC
KICK UP YOUR HEELS
NSIDE SHC 'HODI
YOUR ST   STEP
STEPPIN   TO GO SHOE S'   SHC
PUT YOUR   FOOT FORWARD   HE,
PUT ON YOUR DANCING SHOES   SC
FIT LIKE AN OLD WORN SH   CH

You're MMy Typpe

Show 'em you love 'em...even if you can't spell with this interactive card. Begin with a horizontally folded brown cardstock base; layer with torn tan cardstock strip. Punch holes in rust-colored cardstock strip; reserve punched circles. Affix strip across card front, adding brads for embellishment. Print multiple copies of vintage typewriter clip art onto beige shrink plastic. Punch 1/8" hole in top of each; silhouette cut and shrink according to instructions. Once cool, secure to card with brads. For typewriter, print clip art image onto transparency. Once dry, run through adhesive machine. Punch circles from tan and brown cardstocks. Apply rust, tan and brown circles over keys on sticky side of typewriter. Adhere typewriter to beige cardstock and silhouette cut. Make slits in typewriter for "paper" in front and behind roller. Print sentiment onto cream-colored cardstock. Insert through foremost slit in transparency and small piece behind roller. Mount completed typewriter to card with foam adhesive. Finish with letter stickers.

Torrey Miller, Thornton, Colorado

Supplies: Clip art (Dover Publications); letter stickers (EK Success); transparency; shrink plastic; foam spacers; mini brads; brown, tan, rust, beige and cream cardstocks

Live, Laugh, Love

Warm colors and equally warm sentiments adorn this texture-rich card. Vertically fold a textured brown cardstock base. Layer card front with patterned and embossed papers. Attach brass bookplates and acrylic embellishments by hand stitching with embroidery floss. Thread embroidery floss through small holes in four corners to complete.

Shannon Taylor, Bristol, Tennessee

Supplies: Patterned paper (source unknown); embossed paper (Provo Craft); acrylic license plates (Junkitz); metal bookplates (Anima Designs); embroidery floss (DMC); textured brown cardstock (Bazzill)

The Ocean Holds Its Treasures...

Rawhide-textured paper and warm earthy colors lend a masculine air to this "I love you" card. Begin with a vertically folded cream cardstock base. Round corners of textured paper with a corner punch; layer over card front. Thread buckle onto green ribbon and adhere along left side; accent with small seashells. Create shaker box using a metal frame and beach cut-out. Cut square window into foam core board to fit metal frame; adhere cut-out to back of foam core board. Glue seashells to cut-out and sprinkle cut-out with sand. Enclose by mounting a square-cut portion of a page protector over the foam core, making certain all edges are tightly adhered. Mount metal frame to shaker box base. Print sentiment onto cream-colored cardstock; tear into rectangle, ink edges with brown ink and adhere to card front. Print remainder of sentiment on paper and glue to inside of card to complete.

Deborah March, Lunenburg County, Nova Scotia, Canada

Supplies: Rawhide paper (Provo Craft); ribbon charm and frame (Making Memories); beach cut-out (EK Success); small seashells; sand; brown stamping ink; page protector; tacky tape; cream cardstock

How Do I Love Thee?

Sometimes a simple card isn't an adequate representation of your feelings. Go the extra mile and create a fold-out booklet to house tags that declare your love. See instructions below to re-create card base. Stipple various colors of ink along all edges and folds of pockets and card front. Adhere collage elements randomly on fronts of all pockets and the card itself using a variety of materials including paper ephemera, torn patterned paper, cut-out floral motifs from patterned paper; letter stickers, metal frames, acrylic words, metallic charms, printed twill tape, metal letters, watch parts, miniature glass vials, fiber, fabric, bamboo clips and vellum. Create four customized tags from pre-made tags and patterned papers matted with coordinating colors of cardstock. Punch holes in tops of tags, setting eyelets in some; tie fibers through holes. Secure entire booklet together with ribbon.

Kelly Angard, Highlands Ranch, Colorado

Supplies: Patterned papers (7 Gypsies, Anna Griffin, K & Company, Penny Black, Provo Craft); ephemera tags (Me & My Big Ideas); letter stickers (Wordsworth, K & Company); metal letters, frames and ephemera postage stamps (FoofaLa); best friends frame (Nunn Design); watch pieces, bamboo clip, glass vial (7 Gypsies); letter stamps (Hero Arts); circle punch (Punch Bunch); fibers (Fiber Scraps); star brads (Chatterbox); eyelets; assorted metal charms (source unknown); brown, green, cranberry and beige stamping inks; fabric; ribbon; chipboard; green cardstock

1 Copy pattern provided on page 124. Layer piece of green cardstock with pattern; cut and tear out. Using circle punch, punch half circle and circle as shown in pattern.

2 Score all fold lines using a metal edge ruler and bone folder.

3 Fold top flap down. Accordian-fold and adhere pockets at edges only, to create openings for tags.

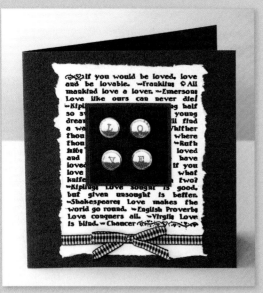

LOVE

Shake up your valentine with mini watch crystal shaker boxes. Vertically fold a red cardstock card base. Stamp quote onto white cardstock, emboss and tear into rectangle. Mat black cardstock square with red cardstock. For shaker box sentiment, stamp letters onto white cardstock; cut into circles to fit inside mini watch crystals. Fill with tiny glass beads; glue each to stamped cardstock circle. Adhere to double-matted square; mount to torn stamped rectangle. Wrap with ribbon bow and affix to card.

Nikki Thompson, Frohna, Missouri

Supplies: Quote stamp (Stampington); letter stamps (Stampendous); mini watch crystals (Scrapworks); stamping ink; clear embossing powder; red and white cardstocks

Love Ya

It's retro. It's kitsch. It's love, 50s style! Start with a vertically folded black cardstock card base. Cover card front with section of textured yellow cardstock. Add strips of red cardstock along right edge and across bottom. Treat edges of yellow and red cardstocks with black ink. Stamp design across bottom red strip and on upper left corner of yellow cardstock. Silhouette cut images or use color copies from vintage magazine and adhere to background. Frame small image with slide mount; affix to bottom of card with foam spacers. Apply acrylic letters on front for sentiment.

Kelly Angard, Highlands Ranch, Colorado

Supplies: Design stamp (EK Success); textured yellow cardstock (Bazzill); slide mount (Anima Designs); letter stickers (K & Company); black stamping ink; vintage magazine images; foam spacers; black and red cardstocks

Love

Personalize this eclectic "I love you" card with a monogrammed tag. The base of this card is vertically folded red cardstock. Cover front of card with patterned paper. Adhere measuring tape embellishments across top and bottom of card front. Tear strip of contrasting piece of patterned paper and chalk torn edges with black chalk. Adhere along bottom half of card front. Stamp square of cream cardstock with vintage image and mat on black cardstock. Punch red cardstock heart. Stamp twill tape with word and adhere to punched heart. Mount heart onto patterned paper square with foam spacer. Punch tag out of patterned paper and stamp with initial stamp. Chalk edges of tag and heart with black chalk. Attach stamped tag, decorative clip, and decorative brad to stamped cardstock square. Adhere to complete.

Valerie Salmon, Carmel, Indiana

Supplies: Patterned papers (Paper Company, 7 Gypsies); vintage stamp (Inkadinkado); fancy letter stamp (Anna Griffin); heart punch (Emagination Crafts); tag punch (EK Success); heart brad, black brad; black and brown stamping inks; black chalk; foam spacers; red and cream cardstocks

All My Love

Open this card to reveal your true feelings to the one you love. Start with a horizontally folded white cardstock base. Using temporary adhesive, mount lavender cardstock to card front. Cut rectangular window through both layers; ink all edges with black ink. Place clear packing tape sticky-side-down onto backside of lavender cardstock, covering window. Turn over and coat packing tape with glitter; tap off excess. Adhere strips of pink paper to front of lavender cardstock; layer with ribbon. Print sentiment onto transparency and emboss; cut into strip and adhere with brads. Accent metal heart with ribbon; affix with foam adhesive. Mount assembly to card front. For card's interior, line with patterned paper. Print and emboss sentiment onto transparency. Cut into rectangle; frame with purple paper frame and adhere to inside of card. Apply dimensional letters so that they show through window.

Denise Tucker, Versailles, Indiana

Supplies: Patterned paper (Chatterbox); metal heart charm (Artistic Expressions); dimensional letters (Colorbök); black stamping ink; ribbon; eyelets; transparency film; packing tape; glitter; foam spacers; lavender, pink and white cardstocks

Love

Sometimes all it takes is a single word to express your true feelings. Begin with a horizontally folded purple cardstock card base. Cut a peach cardstock block and lavender rectangle. Tear a square from peach cardstock; treat edges with purple ink. Layer with a torn, slightly smaller handmade paper square. Cut heart shape from metallic lavender paper. Stamp sentiment onto peach cardstock; tear into strip. Set eyelets in both ends and thread with fiber. Glue handmade paper assembly to left side of card. Layer with heart and strip, securing fibers behind peach cardstock block to secure; mount to card.

Nancy Korf, Portland, Oregon

Supplies: Handmade paper (source unknown); word stamp (DeNami Design); lavender metallic paper (Club Scrap); purple ink; lavender eyelets; fiber; purple and peach cardstocks

Thinking Of You

Watermark stamps create a subtle backdrop for this elegant card. Start with a vertically folded plum cardstock card base. Using watermark ink, stamp image onto green cardstock rectangle slightly smaller than card front; tear bottom edge. Stamp sentiment onto vellum and cut into square. Layer over stamped cardstock; make two parallel cuts at top of vellum, cutting through stamped cardstock. Thread ribbon through slits to form a french knot. Adhere green cardstock to front to complete.

Kneka Smith, Phoenix, Arizona

Supplies: Stamps (Stampin' Up!); watermark and purple stamping inks; vellum; ribbon; plum and green cardstocks

Supplies: Patterned paper (Karen Foster Design); floral stamp (Penny Black); gold embossing powder; embossing ink; refill stamping inks in yellow, gold and green; markers; metal thread; wire; brads; gold rub-ons; glossy white and maroon cardstocks

Life

This beautiful and reflective card could be presented for numerous occasions. Begin with a horizontally folded card base of maroon cardstock. Tear patterned paper in irregular shape; wrap with metallic thread, apply gold ink to edges and mount on card front. Create metallic paper using bottles of gold, green and yellow ink refills on glossy white paper. When dry, cut and mount. Tear sentiment from patterned paper and adhere to card front with foam spacers. Stamp and emboss floral images on vellum and emboss with gold embossing powder. Apply gold rub-on to stamped vellum background; cut and adhere. Repeat stamp on white cardstock and emboss with gold embossing powder. Add marker detail to images; cut out and affix with brads over stamped vellum. Add wire accent to complete.

Joy Candrian, Sandy, Utah

Thinking Of You

Purple hearts seem to pop off the card when framed in metal-rimmed tags. Begin with a vertically folded textured lavender cardstock base. Mount textured dark purple cardstock square and a slightly smaller lavender square to card front; layer with purple mesh and torn patterned paper. Punch paper hearts and affix to metal-rimmed tags. Adhere tags to card front and stamp with sentiment to complete.

Stephanie David, Astorville, Ontario, Canada

Supplies: Patterned paper (Creative Imaginations); phrase stamp (Stampin' Up!); purple mesh; purple stamping ink; metal-rimmed tags (Avery); textured purple and lavender cardstocks (Bazzill)

Thinking Of You

Create a window of opportunity to tell someone you're thinking about him or her. Start with a vertically-folded card base of white cardstock. Stamp and emboss repeated images onto card front. Chalk edges with yellow chalk. Cut two squares from a page protector to create a slide mount window; enclose pressed flowers between layers. Glue slide mount closed. Tie yellow ribbon around slide mount. Cut window in card front slightly larger than opening of slide mount. Adhere slide mount to card front. Stamp and emboss sentiment on inside of card to appear through window.

MaryJo Regier, Memory Makers Books

Supplies: Transparency mount (Design Originals); floral stamp (Magenta); phrase stamp (Stampin' Up!); pressed flowers; yellow ribbon; page protector; maroon stamping ink; clear embossing powder; white cardstock

Supplies: Floral ribbon (Michaels); textured green cardstock (Westrim); textured taupe cardstock (Bazzill); letter stamps (PSX Design); flower punch (Family Treasures); metal-rimmed tag (Making Memories); black stamping ink; ribbon; button

Thinking Of You

A pre-made floral ribbon makes for a pretty accent on this lovely card. Start with a horizontally folded textured taupe cardstock base. Cut rectangle from textured green cardstock; adhere floral ribbon across bottom and tie cream ribbon into bow across top. Stamp sentiment above and below cream ribbon. Stamp word on vellum metal-rimmed tag and adhere over ribbon. Accent with flower punched from green cardstock with button center. Mount assemblage to card front to complete.

Polly McMillan, Bullhead City, Arizona

Thinking Of You

Altered hammered tin adorns this regal card. Begin with a vertically folded card base of black cardstock. See instructions to follow to create tin accents. Mount embossed paper to card front. Print title on transparency and immediately emboss with gold embossing powder. Attach printed transparency to card front with brads. Arrange and adhere finished tin pieces to card front with foam spacers to complete.

Denise Tucker, Versailles, Indiana

Supplies: Embossed tin (Artistic Expressions); embossed paper (Provo Craft); gold leafing kit (Delta); transparency; brads; gold embossing powder; black cardstock

1 Using wire snips, trim embossed tin scrapbook page to extract desired design elements. Paint tin elements with base coat from Renaissance foil leafing kit by Delta. Allow to dry completely.

2 Apply coat of adhesive from kit; let dry. Apply second coat. Allow to dry one hour.

3 Apply foil sheet shiny-side-up onto tin element, rubbing with fingertip to fill all impressions. Peel off sheet. Apply sealer if desired.

Thinking Of You

A rolled-blind effect is an elegant way to reveal a lovely stamp. Begin with a vertically folded textured brown cardstock base. Layer with patterned paper. Stamp image onto cream-colored patterned paper; ink edges and adhere to card front. Stamp sentiment onto shrink plastic; cut to size and punch hole in top. Shrink according to manufacturer's directions. For frame, cut along the interior of three sides of textured brown cardstock rectangle. Roll back center flap, tie back with thread and accent with shrink plastic tag. Adhere over stamped image.

Sheela Zelmer, Quispamis, New Brunswick, Canada

Supplies: Patterned papers and sentiment stamp (Anna Griffin); leaf stamp (Rubber Stampede); poly-shrink plastic (Lucky Squirrel); textured brown cardstock (Bazzill); maroon stamping ink; thread

Remember The Moments

This nostalgic card recalls time gone by. Begin with a vertically folded brown card-stock base. Cut rectangle from patterned paper and tear in half diagonally; treat edges with brown ink and mount on dark brown cardstock. Set eyelets along torn edges; thread with elastic band in zigzag pattern. Print sentiment on cream cardstock, cut to size and affix with brads. Cut tag from cream cardstock; ink edges. Thread button with wire and wrap around bottom of tag. Affix printed twill ribbon diagonally across tag. Further embellish with page dart and fibers; mount with foam adhesive. Treat entire card surface with brown ink. Adhere letter stickers to complete sentiment.

Deanna Hutchison, Langley, British Columbia, Canada

Supplies: Patterned paper (K & Company); elastic, printed twill ribbon (7 Gypsies); page dart; letter stickers (EK Success); eyelets; brads; wire; button; fiber; brown stamping ink; foam spacers; cream, brown and black cardstocks

Thinking Of You

Capture the feeling of fall with this sophisticated card. Start with a vertically folded card base of cream cardstock. Cover card front with beige cardstock and torn strip of ginger-colored cardstock; ink torn edges with brown stamping ink. Cut brown corrugated paper into square and adhere to torn strip. Stamp senti-ment and affix embossed metal tile to corrugated paper with brads.

Candice Cruz, Somerville, Massachusetts

Supplies: Corrugated paper (DMD); phrase stamp (Endless Creations); metal tile (Scrapyard 329); brads; brown stamping ink; beige, ginger and cream-colored cardstocks

Best Of Luck!

This card employs a microscope slide holder that has been altered to exude down-home country charm. Begin with a vertically folded green cardstock base. Layer card front with torn strips of patterned papers, vintage-style ephemera and floral stickers. Treat chipboard microscope slide holder with green inks; adorn with ephemera and stickers. Accent with copper tag embellished with eyelet and gingham ribbon; handwrite sentiment and adhere. Collage additional patterned paper and floral stickers. Cut to size and adhere to microscope slides; seal with copper tape on all sides. Affix slides inside recessed compartments. Mount slide holder at askew angle on card front with foam spacers.

Kari Hansen-Daffin, Memory Makers magazine

Supplies: Microscope slides, slide holder, copper tag (Anima Designs); copper word charms, ephemera (Foofala); copper tape (Sunday International); patterned papers, floral stickers (Anna Griffin); green stamping ink; permanent black marker; foam spacers; gingham ribbon; green cardstock

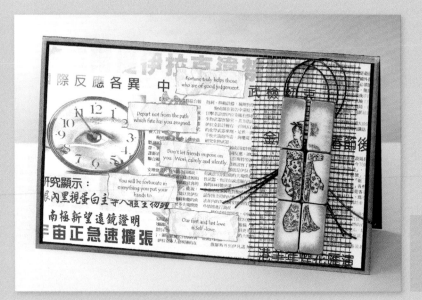

Supplies: Patterned paper (DMD); mini dominoes (Boxer Scrapbook Productions); copper leafing pen (Krylon); paper cord (Yasutomo); Asian stamp (PSX Design); solvent ink (Tsukineko); red stamping ink; clear lacquer; black cardstock

Good Luck

Nothing says "luck" like fortune cookie fortunes. Begin with a horizontally folded black cardstock base. Apply copper leafing pen to edges of card front. Mount with Asian-themed patterned paper; layer card front with crumpled and inked "fortunes" cut from patterned paper and red mesh and red paper cord. For domino embellishment, arrange mini dominoes closely together and stamp with image using solvent-based ink; ink front edges with red ink. Coat dominoes with clear lacquer to seal and allow to dry. Color domino edges with copper leafing pen. Adhere grouping to card front atop mesh to finish.

Jodi Amidei, Memory Makers Books

Blessings

Create the incredible look of batik on regular printer paper—all without the mess! Start with a vertically folded royal blue cardstock base. On printer paper, randomly stamp symbol using beige ink. Emboss all images with clear embossing powder. Crumple paper, flatten and ink with blue, purple and light blue ink pads. Spritz paper with water until inks blend. Let dry. Brush black ink pad over crumples in paper; edge paper with gold leafing pen and mount on card front. Create mat for title in similar fashion but using green, teal and yellow inks. Stamp sentiment on royal blue cardstock; emboss and edge with gold. Mount title onto green mat; adhere to card front. Insert decorative brads under title. "Hang" brass fan charms with metallic thread, adhering fans to card to secure.

Connie Cox, Westminster, Colorado

Supplies: Asian stamp (Plaid); decorative brads (Fiber Scraps); brass fans (Magic Scraps); word stamp (My Sentiments Exactly); gold fibers (Timeless Touches); beige, blue, purple, light blue, green, yellow, teal and black stamping inks; clear and gold embossing powders; gold leafing pen (Krylon); printer paper; royal blue cardstock

Best Wishes

This straightforward card says it all. Start with horizontally folded green textured cardstock square card base. Lightly brush white ink pad over surface of card. Thread green grosgrain ribbon onto ribbon charm and adhere across front of card. Print sentiment on cream cardstock; cut to size and mat with dark green cardstock. Mount sentiment on bottom of card front to complete.

Brandi Ginn, Lafayette, Colorado

Supplies: Ribbon charm (Making Memories); grosgrain ribbon; white stamping ink; green textured cardstock (Bazzill); cream and dark green cardstocks

Congratulations

Don't forget the lucky penny when wishing someone congratulations! Start with a horizontally folded black cardstock card base. Layer with rust-colored cardstock and torn patterned paper. Embellish card with skeletal leaves, vintage dictionary page, typewriter die cuts, mini domino and penny nailhead. Attach label holder over collaged elements. Stamp aluminum label with metal impact letter stamps and rub with solvent-based ink. Secure label with tied ribbons, securing ends in back.

Kari Hansen-Daffin, Memory Makers magazine

Supplies: Patterned paper (Carolee's Creations); penny nail head, label holder (Magic Scraps); aluminum label and vintage dictionary page (Anima Designs); metal impact letter stamps (Making Memories); typewriter die cuts (DMD); skeletal leaves (Nature's Handmade Paper); mini domino (Boxer Scrapbook Productions); black solvent ink (Tsukineko); black brads; gingham ribbon; rust and black cardstocks

Supplies: Patterned papers and letter stickers (Chatterbox); textured green cardstock (Bazzill); page pebble (Making Memories); ribbon

Congratulations

A crisp congratulations card like this is sure to spread cheer to its recipient. Begin with a horizontally folded textured green cardstock base. Layer purple patterned paper with floral patterned paper; mount to card front. Tear strip of purple patterned paper; adhere. Apply letter stickers to purple strip. Adhere acrylic pebble to patterned paper; trim to size and embellish with ribbon bow to complete.

Linda Beeson, Ventura, California

Congratulations

Personalize a congratulations card by adding a photo of the congratulatee! Vertically fold a white cardstock card base. Cover card front with contrasting patterned papers. Stamp title onto twill tape. Mat photo with royal blue cardstock; adhere at askew angle. Secure printed twill tape across photo with decorative eyelets to complete.

Cori Dahmen, Portland, Oregon

Supplies: Patterned papers (Pebbles); alphabet stamps (PSX Design); square eyelets (ScrapArts); twill tape (Creek Bank Creations); stamping ink; white and royal blue cardstocks

Congratulations

Create a classy card that is all at once simple and sophisticated. Horizontally fold lavender cardstock for the card base. Tear right edge of patterned paper and mount on left side of card front. Stamp and emboss sentiment. Accent heart charm with organza ribbon; affix over patterned paper.

Shari Frost-Job, Buffalo, Minnesota

Supplies: Patterned paper (NRN Designs); rubber stamp (www.jodypoesy.com); heart charm (www.upaonscharm.com); stamping ink; silver embossing powder; organza ribbon; lavender cardstock

Congrats

An atractive slide mount shaker box adorns this cheerful card. Begin with a horizontally folded white cardstock base. Layer card front with patterned paper. Cut two pieces of tacky tape; adhere at top and bottom of card and coat with tiny lavender beads. Color twill tape with pink stamping ink; stamp with alphabet stamps and adhere. For shaker element, stamp butterfly with pink ink onto white cardstock square cut to same size as slide mount. Stamp another image with solvent-based ink onto cut piece of transparency. Using two layers of foam tape, sandwich loose beads between cardstock and transparency squares so that stamped images align. Affix slide mount and adhere assembly to card front to finish.

Jennifer Ingle, Aurora, Colorado

Supplies: Patterned paper (Colors by Design); slide mount (Magic Scraps); coordinating rubber stamps (Stampin' Up!); alphabet stamps (PSX Design); black solvent ink (Tsukineko); pink stamping ink; twill tape, tacky tape, beads; foam tape; white cardstock

With Sympathy

This lovely card can be assembled easily thanks to pre-made elements. Start with a vertically folded card base of green cardstock. Adhere fiber mesh at askew angle on card front. Tie premade tag with fiber. Adhere across card front. Stamp sentiment on bottom of card. Layer with acrylic pebble to complete.

Cori Dahmen, Portland, Oregon

Supplies: Fiber mesh (ScrapArts); tag (Dolphin Enterprises); phrase stamp (Anna Griffin); acrylic pebble (Creative Imaginations); fibers (Fiber Scraps); black stamping ink; green cardstock

With Sympathy

Here ink accents add soft detail to this pretty card. Begin with a square card base of vertically folded white cardstock. Mount strip of maroon cardstock along left edge of card front. Layer with strip of patterned paper that has been torn on one side. Cut pink paper rectangle and adhere at askew angle on card front. Stamp image on white cardstock and add color with inking pad ink. Mat stamped image with maroon cardstock and adhere. Stamp sentiment on white cardstock, cut to size and mat with green cardstock; adhere with foam adhesive. Poke two holes through top left front of card; thread fiber through and tie into bow. Thread beads onto fiber ends and knot.

Cori Dahmen, Portland, Oregon

Supplies: Patterned and pink papers (Colorbök); flower and phrase stamp (Stampin' Up!); fiber (Fiber Scraps); black stamping ink; pink, blue and green stamping inks; beads; foam spacers; maroon and white cardstocks

With Sympathy

Express your condolences with this simply elegant card. Begin with a vertically folded white cardstock base. Adhere pre-made flower sticker to black cardstock rectangle; adhere to card front. Stamp sentiment on white cardstock and tear to size; ink edges and mount. Adhere pre-made metal corners to black cardstock rectangle to complete.

Jill Tennyson, Lafayette, Colorado

Supplies: Metal corners (Making Memories); pre-made flower sticker (EK Success); phrase stamp (Savvy Stamps); black stamping ink; white and black cardstocks

Supplies: Double-sided patterned paper, ribbon charm (Making Memories); colored brads (Karen Foster Design); flower stickers (Miss Elizabeth); ribbon; lavender vellum; lavender cardstock

In Your Time Of Sorrow

Here soft colors help to extend heartfelt wishes. Create the card base from horizontally folded, two-sided patterned paper. Print sentiment and verse on lavender vellum; layer over entire card. Thread ribbon charm onto lavender ribbon and adhere across top of card front. Print title on lavender cardstock, cut into tag shape and punch hole at top. Chalk edges with lavender chalk and adorn with translucent stickers. Thread ribbon through tag and adhere horizontally. Tear lavender cardstock and slide behind quote; secure with colored brads.

Kathy Fesmire, Athens, Tennessee

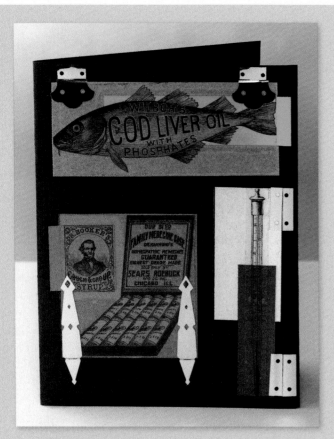

Cod Liver Oil

This nostalgic peekaboo card is sure to lift the spirits of someone who's "under the weather." Start by vertically folding black cardstock to create base. Cut three windows with craft knife, leaving one side of each window uncut. Fold each window flap along its uncut edge to create crease. Mount various-colored cardstock shapes on window flaps; adhere vintage clip art images printed onto transparency film over each prepared flap. Add decorative faux-brass hinge stickers. Finish by placing cardstock that has been printed with "Get Well Soon" behind the windows. Chalk sentiment to add dimension.

Torrey Miller, Thornton, Colorado

Supplies: Hinge stickers (Creek Bank Creations); vintage clip art (Dover Publications); black, blue, green, red, yellow, purple and oatmeal cardstocks; transparency film; chalk

Supplies: Periwinkle and yellow patterned papers (Lasting Impressions); green patterned paper (Pebbles); flower eyelets (www.eyeletqueen.com); letter stamps (Hero Arts, PSX Design); green raffia, label holder, trim (Magic Scraps); flower punch (EK Success); watch charm (www.maudeandmillie. com); colored brads; buttons; black stamping ink

Get Well Soon

Spread surefire cheer with this bright card. Start with a horizontally folded card base of periwinkle patterned paper. Cut rectangle from green patterned paper and affix to card front with flower eyelets. Punch flowers from yellow patterned paper. Adhere metal-rimmed tag, punched flowers accented with buttons and small yellow rectangle to card front. Stamp sentiment. Layer yellow rectangle with label holder affixed with colored brads. Adhere watch charm to bottom right corner. Tie raffia bow across top of card. Affix trim across bottom of card to complete.

Polly McMillan, Bullhead City, Arizona

Get Well Soon!

This whimsical and dimensional card is bound to be the bearer of good feelings. Begin with a horizontally folded green cardstock base. Adhere patterned paper to card front. Apply letter stickers to create sentiment. For butterfly accent, dry emboss a copper sheet into shape based upon a die cut. Paint copper butterfly with several coats of alcohol paints. Once paint is dry, lightly sand. Apply thin coat of pigment powder to black butterfly die cut. Adhere die cut over brass butterfly. Dip silver brads in yellow alcohol ink to color and affix to corners of card front.

Michelle Pendleton, Colorado Springs, Colorado

Supplies: Patterned paper, letter stickers (Creative Imaginations); butterfly die cut (Li'l Davis Designs); copper sheet (AMACO); alcohol paints (Jacquard); pigment powders and medium (Ranger); square mini brads; sandpaper; green cardstock

Get Well

This pretty, fluttery card is sure to lift spirits. Start with a horizontally folded card base of blue cardstock. Mat light blue cardstock with orange cardstock and mount on card front. Cut two parallel slits in center of card front near bottom. Thread ribbon through. Using a craft knife, cut butterflies from patterned paper; adhere at random, leaving wings free. For 3-D effect, gently bend wings away from bodies.

Emily Curry Hitchingham, Memory Makers Books

Supplies: Patterned paper (PSX Design); ribbon, blue, orange and light blue cardstocks

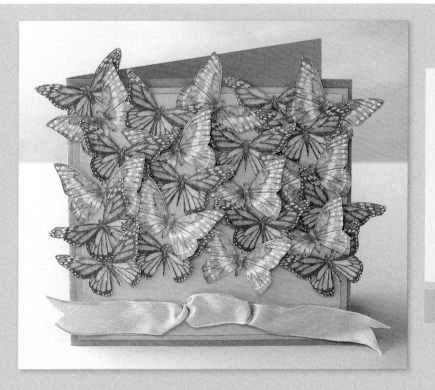

Thanks

Make a thank-you card that has real "charm." Begin with a horizontally folded textured orange cardstock base. Treat edges of card with brown stamping ink. Print title onto patterned paper; cut, ink edges and sew onto textured blue cardstock with sewing machine. Ink edges of blue cardstock. Knot blue ribbon and attach to blue cardstock across patterned paper with bar conchos. Affix charm to ribbon with jump ring. Adhere assemblage to lower half of card front.

Janet Hopkins, Frisco, Texas

Supplies: Patterned paper (Chatterbox); flower charm (source unknown); bar conchos (Scrapworks); textured blue and orange cardstocks (Bazzill); ribbon; jump ring; brown stamping ink

Merci Beaucoup

Create an international sensation with this "tres chic" card. Start with a vertically folded, speckled white cardstock base. Trim approximately 1" from right edge of card front. Print out Eiffel Tower clip art and title on white cardstock; cut both to size. Treat edges and surface of clip art and title with black and light blue inks. Mat clip art on textured black cardstock. Affix clip art and title with staples. Cover interior of card with blue gingham patterned paper. Add tiny safety pin to clip art to complete.

Tracy Kuethe, Milford, Ohio

Supplies: Speckled cardstock (Wassau Paper); textured black cardstock (Bazzill); patterned paper (Making Memories); clip art; blue and black inks; staples; safety pin

Supplies: Patterned paper (Karen Foster Design); mesh (Jest Charming); letter stickers (EK Success); chalk; brads; yellow cardstock; fibers

Thanks

Add dimension and texture to create a striking salutation of thanks. Start with a vertically folded card base of yellow cardstock. Cut rectangle of patterned paper slightly smaller than card front, tear off top edge and mount. Weave a variety of fibers in and out of faux metal mesh; adhere. Attach chalked letter stickers to card front with brads to complete.

Lisa Dixon, East Brunswick, New Jersey

Thank You

Industrial meets kitsch in this fun thank you-card. Begin with a horizontally folded textured green cardstock base. Mount patterned paper to front of card. Ink edges of shipping tag with brown ink and stamp with sentiment. Thread with fibers and adhere at askew angle. Attach photo turns to card front with snaps. Stamp cancellation mark image on white cardstock; treat with brown stamping ink. Adhere to frame and mount to finish.

Shari Frost-Job, Buffalo, Minnesota

Supplies: Patterned paper (KI Memories); photo turns and snaps (Making Memories); phrase stamp (Junque); cancellation stamp (www.maudeandmillie.com); fibers; shipping tag; green and brown stamping inks; textured green cardstock (Bazzill)

Thanks!

Sometimes just a simple "thanks" is all you need. Begin with a tall, vertically folded white cardstock base. Cover top third of card front with blue cardstock. Cover remainder with orange cardstock. Cut strip of patterned paper; adhere across card front. Punch flower from green cardstock. Add detail with fine-tip marker. Adhere flower to patterned strip; thread button and affix to center of flower. Stamp sentiment at lower right corner to complete.

Melissa Deakin, Williamsville, New York

Supplies: Patterned paper (KI Memories); flower punch (EK Success); letter stamps (PSX Design); black ink; black marker; button; thread; white, blue, orange and green cardstocks

Thanks

Beautiful embossed paper creates a dramatic backdrop for a heartfelt thank you. Start with a horizontally folded black cardstock base. Mat embossed white paper with pink cardstock. Paint metal label holder with white acrylic paint; let dry. Sand gently and dab with black ink. Adhere woven word label on embossed paper; position label holder over woven label. Thread thin black ribbon through holes and knot; secure ends under mat and mount to card front.

Denise Tucker, Versailles, Indiana

Supplies: Embossed paper (Provo Craft); metal label holder (Making Memories); woven label (Me & My Big Ideas); white acrylic paint; black stamping ink; sandpaper; black and pink cardstocks

Thanks

Free-formed wire and an accordion-folded sentiment add dimension to this attractive card. Start with a long, horizontally folded sage cardstock base. Cover card front with sand-colored cardstock. Tear four strips of textured brown cardstock and layer over top and bottom of sand cardstock; roll torn edges. Rub metallic chalk onto textured cardstock; set two tiny eyelets on top and three on bottom. Thread with wire and twist into free-form shapes. Print sentiment onto sage cardstock and cut into long strip; accordion-fold. Chalk creases of title strip and affix with brads.

Deanna Hutchison, Langley, British Columbia, Canada

Supplies: Textured brown cardstock (Bazzill); metallic chalk (Craf T); mini eyelets; brads; wire; sand and sage cardstocks

Many Thanks

Here warm colors and crisp composition combine for a pretty card. Start with a rectangle of navy cardstock. Stamp image with multicolored ink pad onto speckled beige cardstock. Stamp title on top left corner. Add eyelets and tiny navy cardstock square accents under sentiment. Mat with raspberry-colored cardstock and mount onto navy background.

Tara Bazata, Thornton, Colorado

Supplies: Stamps and stamping ink (Stampin' Up!); eyelets; red, navy and beige speckled cardstocks

Thanks

Intricate paper piercing adds subtle beauty to this Asian-themed card. Begin with a tall card base of vertically folded dark green ribbed cardstock. Using temporary adhesive, adhere bamboo pattern to card front. Pierce along design outline with large needle or piercing tool at 1/8" intervals. Remove pattern. Stamp symbol onto card front and emboss with gold embossing powder. Tie Asian coins and charms on fiber. Gather fibers and tie around fold of card, allowing coins and charms to dangle. Complete card with traditional Japanese handmade signature stamp in lower right corner.

Andrea Lyn Vetten-Marley, Aurora, Colorado

Supplies: Asian symbol stamp (source unknown); bamboo pattern (Gerri Sorkin); fibers (Fiber Scraps); Asian coins and charms (Boxer Scrapbook Productions); Japanese handmade stamp (source unknown); dark green ribbed cardstock (Bazzill); red and embossing inks; gold embossing powder

Supplies: Metallic gold cardstock (DMD); silverware stamp (All Night Media); embossing ink; silver embossing powder; vellum; sand and black cardstocks

Thank You For Dinner

Thank gracious hosts with this fun thank-you card. Begin with a vertically folded sand-colored cardstock base. Mat metallic gold cardstock on black cardstock and adhere to card front. Stamp and emboss silverware image on black cardstock, cut and mat with sand cardstock. Print sentiment on vellum; tear and mount across bottom of card.

Oksanna Pope, Los Gatos, California

Sentiments

A beautifully crafted handmade card clearly says "thoughtfulness." However, a just-right sentiment provides a special added touch to speak to the heart of your card's recipient. Look to these helpful sayings when wording your emotions and warm wishes.

Seasons Greetings

We give thanks for unknown blessings already on their way. - Ritual chant

Not what we say about our blessings, but how we use them, is the true measure of our thanksgiving. - W.T. Purkiser

Christmas waves a magical wand over this world, and behold, everything is softer and more beautiful. - Norman Vincent Peale

Blessed is the season which engages the whole world in a conspiracy of love. - Hamilton Wright Mabi

The best of all gifts around any Christmas tree: the presence of a happy family all wrapped up in each other. - Burton Hillis of *Better Homes and Gardens*

Peace on earth will come to stay, when we live Christmas every day. - Helen Steiner Rice

Whatever else be lost among the years, let us keep Christmas a shining thing. - Grace Noll Crowell

May love and light fill your home and heart at Hanukkah. - Sentiments by Versalog

Shalom, peace to you at Hanukkah and always. - Sentiments by Versalog

As you celebrate the Festival of Lights, may your home be bright with happiness and love. - Sentiments by Versalog

Birthday

Youth has no age. - Pablo Picasso

Every year's a souvenir. - Billy Joel

Birthdays are good for you. The more you have the longer you live. - Unknown

You're not getting older, you're getting better. - Unknown

We are always the same age inside. - Gertrude Stein

A birthday is just the first day of another 365-day journey around the sun. Enjoy the trip! - Unknown

Friendship

A friend is one who knows us, but loves us anyway. - Fr. Jerome Cummings

A friend is someone with whom you dare to be yourself. - Frank Crane

A friend might well be reckoned the masterpiece of nature. - Ralph Waldo Emerson

The best mirror is an old friend. - George Herbert

A friend is a gift you give yourself. - Robert Louis Stevenson

A real friend is one who walks in when the rest of the world walks out. - Walter Winchell

My best friend is the one who brings out the best in me. - Henry Ford

Good friends are good for your health. - Irwin Sarason

General Warm Wishes

You're on my mind and in my heart. - Sentiments by Versalog

May love and happiness be today's gifts to you. - Sentiments by Versalog

Haply I think on thee. - William Shakespeare

Sprinkle joy. - Ralph Waldo Emerson

The earth laughs in flowers. - ee cummings

Write it on your heart that every day is the best day of the year. - Ralph Waldo Emerson

Dance like no one is watching. Sing like no one is listening. Love like you've never been hurt and live like it's heaven on earth. - Mark Twain

Remember that happiness is a way of travel, not a destination. - Roy Goodman

Love

Love does not consist in gazing at each other, but in looking outward together in the same direction. - Antoine de Saint Exupery

The best and most beautiful things in the world cannot be seen or even touched-they must be felt with the heart. - Helen Keller

Some love lasts a lifetime. True love lasts forever. - Unknown

Love is not something you feel. It's something you do. - David Wilkerson

Real love stories never have endings. - Richard Bach

Love is composed of a single soul inhabiting two bodies. - Aristotle

Draw a circle, not a heart around the one you love, because a heart can break but a circle lasts forever. - Unknown

Love is a canvas furnished by nature and embroidered by the imagination. - Voltair

You complete me. - Tom Cruise in "Jerry Maguire"

Postal Info

Before you slip your handcrafted creation into the mailbox, be sure that you weigh the card and its envelope together so you won't see it return to you bearing unsightly insufficient-postage stamps. Should your card and envelope exceed the standard first-class 1-oz. postage fee, you'll need to adjust postage accordingly.

First-Class Mail Rates:

First ounce: $0.37

Each additional ounce: $0.23 (includes postcards, letters, large envelopes and small packages)

Maximum weight is 13 ounces

Pieces over 13 ounces can be sent priority mail

Minimum size for first-class mail is 5" long, 3½" high and 0.007" thick

Non Machinable Surcharges:

An additional $0.12 is required for items weighing 1 ounce or less with the following criteria:

Square letters of any size

Height exceeding 6⅛"

Length exceeding 11½"

Thickness exceeding ¼"

Clasps, strings, buttons or similar decorative closure devices that cause the thickness of the item to be uneven

Information from www.usps.com

page 103

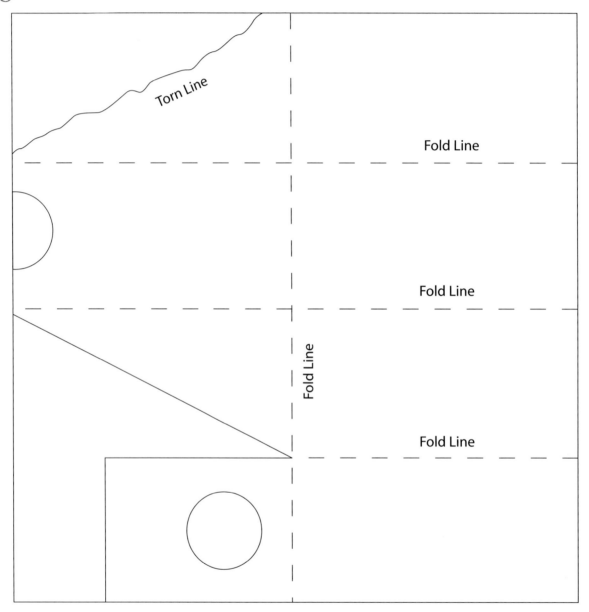

Pattern shown at 51% of original

page 40 Copyright Nancy R. Walker
Pattern shown at 79% of original

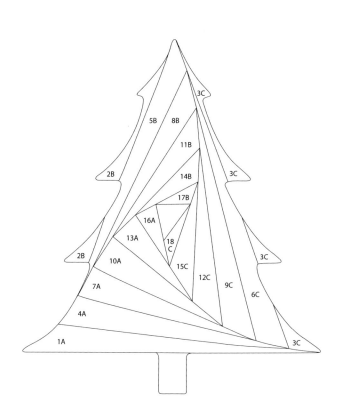

Envelope Template

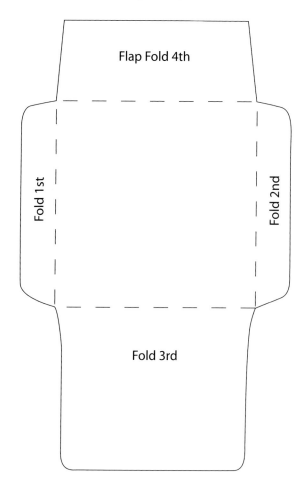

Enlarge patterns to desired card size.

Envelope Template

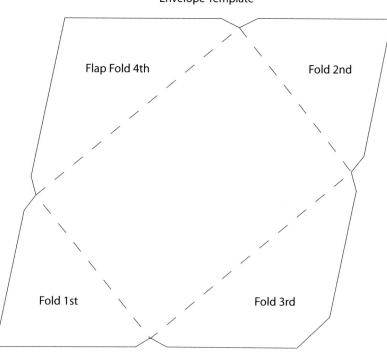

Additional Credits and Sources

Page 3 Bookplate

Create envelope from patterned paper using a template. Line interior with coordinating patterned paper. Treat edges with green ink. Craft card by folding coordinating patterned paper in half; wrap crease with fibers strung with beads and insert.

Jodi Amidei, Memory Makers Books

Supplies: Envelope pattern (Hot Off the Press); patterned paper (Paper Adventures); beads (Westrim); fibers; ink

Web Sites:

Emotions Greeting Cards
www.emotionscards.com/museum/history.html

Famous Quotes
www.famousquotes.com

House of Quotes
www.houseofquotes.com

Rubber Stamping Resource by Donovan www.bydonovan.com/sayings.html

The Greeting Card Association www.greetingcard.org/gcindustry_whoissending.html

United States Postal Service www.usps.com

Versalog www.versalog.com/v/

Sources

The following companies manufacture products featured in this book. Please check your local retailers to find these materials. In addition, we have made every attempt to properly credit the items mentioned in this book. We apologize to any company that we have listed incorrectly or the sources were unknown, and we would appreciate hearing from you.

100 Proof Press, Inc.
(740) 594-2315
www.100proofpress.com

3M Stationery
(800) 364-3577
www.3m.com

7 Gypsies
(800) 588-6707
www.7gypsies.com

Accu-Cut® (wholesale only)
(800) 288-1670
www.accucut.com

Adobe
www.adobe.com

All My Memories
(888) 553-1998
www.allmymemories.com

All Night Media—see Plaid Enterprises

American Art Clay Company (AMACO)
(800) 374-1600
www.amaco.com

American Crafts
(801) 226-0747
www.americancrafts.com

American Greetings
(216) 252-7300
www.americangreetings.com

American Tag Company
(800) 223-3956
www.americantag.net

American Traditional Designs®
(800) 448-6656
www.americantraditional.com

Angelwings Enterprises
(800) 400-3717
www.radiantpearls.com

Anima Designs
(800) 570-6847
www.animadesigns.com

Anna Griffin, Inc. (wholesale only)
(888) 817-8170
www.annagriffin.com

Artistic Expressions
(219) 764-5158
www.artisticexpressionsinc.com

Auto FX Software
(205) 980-1121
www.autofx.com

Autumn Leaves
(800) 588-6707
www.autumnleaves.com

Avery Dennison Corporation
(800) GO-AVERY
www.avery.com

Bazzill Basics Paper
(480) 558-8557
www.bazzillbasics.com

Biblical Impressions
(877) 587-0941
www.biblical.com

Blue Moon Beads
(800) 377-6715
www.bluemoonbeads.com

Bo-Bunny Press
(801) 771-0481
www.bobunny.com

Boxer Scrapbook Productions
(503) 625-0455
www.boxerscrapbooks.com

Brother Sister Design Studio—no info available

Buttons Galore
(856) 753-0165
www.buttonsgaloreandmore.com

Canson, Inc.®
(800) 628-9283
www.canson-us.com

Card Connection, The
—see Michaels

Cardeaux®, a division of Laser Works, Inc.
(800) 226-8905
www.lwipromo.com

Carl Mfg. USA, Inc.
(800) 257-4771
www.Carl-Products.com

Carolee's Creations®
(435) 563-1100
www.carolees.com

Chatterbox, Inc.
(208) 939-9133
www.chatterboxinc.com

Clearsnap, Inc.
(800) 448-4862
www.clearsnap.com

Close To My Heart®
(888) 655-6552
www.closetomyheart.com

Club Scrap™
(888) 634-9100
www.clubscrap.com

Coats & Clark
(800) 648-1479
www.coatsandclark.com

Colorbök™, Inc. (wholesale only)
(800) 366-4660
www.colorbok.com

Colors by Design
(800) 832-8436
www.colorsbydesign.com

Coronado Island Stamping
(629) 477-8900
www.cistamping.com

Crafter's Workshop, The
(877) CRAFTER
www.thecraftersworkshop.com

Craf-T Products
(507) 235-3996
www.craf-tproducts.com

Creative Imaginations (wholesale only)
(800) 942-6487
www.cigift.com

Creative Impressions
(719) 596-4860
www.creativeimpressions.com

Creek Bank Creations, Inc.
(217) 427-5980
www.creekbankcreations.com

Current®, Inc.
(800) 848-2848
www.currentinc.com

Cut-It-Up™
(530) 389-2233
www.scrapamento.com

Darcie's Country Folk
(800) 453-1527
www.darcie.com

Darice, Inc.
(800) 321-1494
www.darice.com

Delta Technical Coatings, Inc.
(800) 423-4135
www.deltacrafts.com

Deluxe Designs
(480) 497-9005
www.deluxecuts.com

DeNami Design Rubber Stamps
(253) 437-1626
www.denamidesign.com

Derwent Cumberland Pencil Co.
www.pencils.co.uk

Design Originals
(800) 877-7820
www.d-originals.com

DMC Corp.
(973) 589-0606
www.dmc.com

DMD Industries, Inc. (wholesale only)
(800) 805-9890
www.dmdind.com

Dolphin Enterprises
(800) 782-6748
www.protect-a-page.com

Doodlebug Design Inc.™
(801) 966-9952
www.doodlebugdesigninc.com

Dover Publications, Inc.
(800) 223-3130
www.doverpublications.com

Duncan Enterprises
(800) 782-6748
www.duncancrafts.com

Dymo
www.dymo.com

Effie Fitzfinger—no info available

Eggery Place, The
www.theeggeryplace.com

EK Success™, Ltd. (wholesale only)
(800) 524-1349
www.eksuccess.com

Ellison™ Craft & Design
(800) 253-2238
www.ellison.com

Emagination Crafts, Inc. (wholesale only)
(630) 833-9521
www.emaginationcrafts.com

Endless Creations, Inc.
(920) 405-9390
www.endlesscreationsrubberstamps.com

Eyelets Etc.™
(303) 921-0476
www.eyelets-etc.com

Family Archives, The
(888) 622-6556
www.heritagescrapbooks.com

Family Treasures, Inc.®
www.familytreasures.com

Fiber Scraps
(215) 230-4905
www.fiberscraps.com

Fiskars, Inc. (wholesale only)
(715) 842-2091
www.fiskars.com

FLAX art & design
(415) 552-2355
www.flaxart.com

FoofaLa
(402) 330-3208
www.foofala.com

Frances Meyer, Inc.®
(800) 372-6237
www.francesmeyer.com

Generations—no info available

Gerri Sorkin—no info available

Golden Artist Colors, Inc.
(800) 959-6543
www.goldenacrylics.com

Golden Oak Papers
(509) 325-5456

Graphic Products Corporation
(800) 323-1660
www.gpcpapers.com

Halcraft USA
(212) 376-1580
www.halcraft.com

Hampton Art Stamps, Inc.
(800) 229-1019
www.hamptonart.com

Happy Hammer, The
(303) 690-3883
www.thehappyhammer.com

Heritage Handcrafts
(303) 683-0963

Hero Arts® Rubber Stamps, Inc. (wholesale only)
(800) 822-4376
www.heroarts.com

Hobby Lobby Stores, Inc.
www.hobbylobby.com

Holly Berry House
(800) 735-2752
www.hollyberryhouse.com

Home Depot U.S.A., Inc.
www.homedepot.com

Hot Off The Press, Inc.
(800) 227-9595
www.paperpizazz.com

Hy-Ko Products
(800) 292-0550
www.hy-ko.com

Inkadinkado® Rubber Stamps
(800) 888-4652
www.inkadinkado.com

Jacquard Products/Rupert, Gibbon
& Spider, Inc.
(800) 442-0455
www.jacquardproducts.com

Jasc Software
(800) 622-2793
www.jasc.com

Jennifer Collection, The
(518) 272-4572
www.paperdiva.net

Jesse James & Co., Inc.
(610) 435-0201
www.jessejamesbutton.com

Jest Charming
(702) 564-5101
www.jestcharming.com

Jo-Ann Fabric & Crafts
(888) 739-4120
www.joann.com

Joan Farber—no info available

Junkitz™
(732) 792-1108
www.junkitz.com

Junque
www.junque.net

Just For Fun® Rubber Stamps
(717) 938-9898
www.jffstamps.com

K & B Innovations, Inc.
(262) 966-0305
www.shrinkydinks.com

K & Company
(888) 244-2083
www.kandcompany.com

Kangaroo & Joey®, Inc.
(800) 646-8065
www.kangarooandjoey.com

Karen Foster Design™
(wholesale only)
(801) 451-9779
www.karenfosterdesign.com

KI Memories
(469) 633-9665
www.kimemories.com

Krylon
(216) 566-2000
www.krylon.com

Lasting Impressions for Paper, Inc.
(801) 298-1979
www.lastingimpressions.com

Li'l Davis Designs
(949) 838-0344
www.lildavisdesigns.com

Limited Edition Rubber Stamps
(650) 594-4242
www.LimitedEditionRS.com

Lowe's Companies, Inc.
(800) 44-LOWES
www.lowes.com

Lucky Squirrel
(00) 462-4912
www.luckysquirrel.com

Magenta Rubber Stamps
(wholesale only)
(800) 565-5254
www.magentarubberstamps.com

Magic Scraps™
(972) 238-1838
www.magicscraps.com

Making Memories
(800) 286-5263
www.makingmemories.com

Marcel Schurman
(800) 333-6724
www.schurmanfinepapers.com

Ma Vinci's Reliquary
www.crafts.dm.net

May Arts
www.mayarts.com

McGill, Inc.
(800) 982-9884
www.mcgillinc.com

me & my BiG ideas®
(wholesale only)
(949) 583-2065
www.meandmybigideas.com

Meri Meri
www.merimeri.com

Michaels® Arts & Crafts
(800) MICHAELS
www.michaels.com

Miss Elizabeth—no info available

MOD (my own design)
(303) 641-8680
www.mod-myowndesign.com

Mrs. Grossman's Paper Co.
(wholesale only)
(800) 429-4549
www.mrsgrossmans.com

Museum of Modern Rubber (MOMR)
(865) 587-9991
www.modernrubber.com

My Sentiments Exactly
(719) 260-6001
www.sentiments.com

Nature's Handmade Paper, LLC
(800) 861-7050
www.natureshandmadepaper.com

Nema Ink—no info available

NRN Designs
(800) 421-6958
www.nrndesigns.com

Nunn Design
(360) 379-3557
www.nunndesign.com

Offray
www.offray.com

Paper Adventures®
(wholesale only)
(800) 727-0699
www.paperadventures.com

Paper Candy
www.papercandy.com

Paper Company™, The
www.anwcrestwood.com

Paper Garden, Inc.
(435) 867-6398
www.mypapergarden.com

Paper House Productions
(800) 255-7316
www.paperhouseproductions.com

Paper Illuzionz
(406) 234-8716
www.paperilluzionz.com

Paper Patch®, The
(800) 397-2737
www.paperpatch.com

Paula Best and Co. Rubber Stamps
(831) 632-0587
www.paulabest.com

Pebbles, Inc.
(800) 438-8153
www.pebblesinc.com

Penny Black Inc.
(510) 849-1883
www.pennyblackinc.com

Pilot Pen Corporation of America
(203) 377-8800
www.pilotpen.com

Pioneer Photo Albums, Inc.®
(800) 366-3686
www.pioneerphotoalbums.com

Plaid Enterprises, Inc.
(800) 842-4197
www.plaidonline.com

Polyform Products Co.
(847) 427-0020
www.sculpey.com

Provo Craft® (wholesale only)
(888) 577-3545
www.provocraft.com

PSX Design™
(800) 782-6748
www.psxdesign.com

Punch Bunch, The
(254) 791-4209
www.thepunchbunch.com

QuicKutz®
(888) 702-1146
www.quickutz.com

Ranger Industries, Inc.
(800) 244-2211
www.rangerinc.com

River City Rubber Works
(877) 735-BARN
www.rivercityrubberworks.com

Rollabind LLC
(800) 438-3542
www.rollabind.com

Rubber Stampede
(800) 423-4135
www.rubberstampede.com

Rusty Pickle
(801) 272-2280
www.rustypickle.com

Sakura of America
(800) 776-6257
www.sakuraofamerica.com

Sandylion Sticker Designs
(800) 387-4215
www.sandylion.com

Savvy Stamps
(360) 833-4555
www.savvystamps.com

ScrapArts
(503) 631-4893
www.scraparts.com

Scrap Pagerz™
(435) 645-0696
www.scrappagerz.com

ScrapTherapy Designs, Inc.
(800) 333-7880
www.scraptherapy.com

Scrapworks, LLC
(801) 363-1010
www.scrapworksllc.com

Scrapyard 329
(775) 829-1118
www.scrapyard329.com

SEI, Inc.
(800) 333-3279
www.shopsei.com

Sizzix
(866) 742-4447
www.sizzix.com

Staedtler, Inc.
(800) 927-7723
www.staedtler-usa.com

Stampabilities®
(800) 888-0321
www.stampabilities.com

Stamp Craft- see Plaid Enterprises

Stamp Doctor, The
(208) 286-7644
www.stampdoctor.com

Stampendous!®
(800) 869-0474
www.stampendous.com

Stampin' Up!®
(800) 782-6787
www.stampinup.com

Stampington & Company
(877) STAMPER
www.stampington.com

Stamp Oasis
(702) 880-6474
www.stampoasis.com

Staples, Inc.
(800) 3STAPLE
www.staples.com

Sticker Studio™
(208) 322-2465
www.stickerstudio.com

Strathmore Papers
(800) 628-8816
www.strathmoreartist.com

Sunday International
(800) 401-8644
www.sundayint.com

Suze Weinberg Design Studio
(732) 761-2400
www.schmoozewithsuze.com

Sweetwater
(800) 359-3094
www.sweetwaterscrapbook.com

Timeless Touches/Dove Valley
Productions, LLC
(623) 362-8285
www.timelesstouches.net

Toybox Rubber Stamps
(707) 431-1400
www.toyboxrubberstamps.com

Treehouse Designs
(501) 372-1109
www.treehouse-designs.com

Tsukineko®, Inc.
(800) 769-6633
www.tsukineko.com

Tumblebeasts Stickers
(505) 323-5554
www.tumblebeasts.com

Turtle Press
(206) 706-3186
www.turtlearts.com

Two Busy Moms- see Deluxe Designs

USArtQuest
(800) 200-7848
www.usartquest.com

Wasau Papers
www.wasaupapers.com

Westrim® Crafts
(800) 727-2727
www.westrimcrafts.com

Wilton Enterprises
(630) 810-2205
www.wilton.com

Wintech International Corp.
(800) 263-6043
www.wintechint.com

Wordsworth
(719) 282-3495
www.wordsworthstamps.com

Wrights® Ribbon Accents
(877) 597-4448
www.wrights.com

Xpedx
www.xpedx.com

Xyron®
(800) 793-3523
www.xyron.com

Yasutomo and Company
(650) 737-8888
www.yasutomo.com

Index